I0430185

Secrets Revealed:
Terrorism, USA

WILLIS A. BULLARD

Editor: Becca Hamilton Gossman

Copyright © 2014 Willis A. Bullard

All rights reserved.

ISBN-13: 978-1500527235

ISBN-10: 1500527238

DEDICATION

To my lovely bride – "Prudencia" – forever yours.

ACKNOWLEDGMENTS

I offer a great "Thank You" to the brave men and women of our military; the Freedom fighters of yesterday, today, and tomorrow. Especially Reaper Platoon (LT Bullard and SFC Farmer) - "Fear the Reaper"

God Bless our brothers and sisters working 24/7 securing our borders – the United States Border Patrol Agent (USBP)

And a heartfelt thanks to my editor, Rebecca Hamilton Gossman. A great friend and woman of virtue.

PROLOGUE

There are millions and of people in this world that are suffering from poverty and hoping for a better way of life. Churches, and church-related agencies travel the globe to assist in feeding, housing, and providing medical care for the most destitute of citizens of our world. And although we paint a picture in our own minds of all this taking place in Africa or Asia, we are actually seeing these deplorable conditions here in the Western Hemisphere. Right now, July 2014, there are thousands of children that are crossing the border between the United States of America and Mexico in hopes of finding a safe place to live; in hopes of securing a better life.

Some think that blame should be placed on the Obama administration's misinterpretation of the provisions set forth in the DREAM (Development, Relief, and Education for Alien Minors) Act introduced in 2001 and rewritten almost annually since then. This legislation acts as an amnesty program for illegal aliens that have "done well" during their time in America. For example, a child who comes to America because the parents crossover illegally is allowed to go to school and if he or she graduates high school, they qualify for a 6 year long path to citizenship with the completion of a college degree or two years of military service (www.dreamact.info). There is so much more to this program but it really is not the focus here.

The confusion that has lead us to the humanitarian crisis on the border was created on June 15, 2012, when President Barack Hussein Obama announced that his administration would stop deporting young illegal aliens who match certain criteria previously proposed under the DREAM Act. Naturally, news stations in Central America started to announce the U.S. would not deport anyone under eighteen years of age and left out the criteria necessary to meet the DREAM act standards. Therein lies the big problem. Our understaffed Customs and Border Patrol (CBP) agency is now faced with a surge of illegal immigrants crossing into U.S. territory through our porous borders. So great are the numbers that we are now experiencing a humanitarian crisis the likes of which America has never seen.

Children as young as four years old have been crossing the border and intercepted by CBP and local law enforcement officers. Some of them crossing with no adult traveling with them. These children, much to the surprise of the ignorant masses, are not just Mexican nationals. These children are coming from as far away as El Salvador, Guatemala, and Honduras (considered the most dangerous country in the world 2012 – present).

But let me tell you the scariest part of this mass exodus into America by these children and some of their parents! It is a ruse! I know what you are thinking, this is real and these people are really seeking hope in the land of the free. Please do not be so naïve. That is what the unseen enemy wants us to believe. The media continues to portray the mass exodus from Central America as an escape from crime and gang violence. However the president of Guatemala has already come forward to say this was not true and that these families were promised safe passage into the United States with the assurance that U.S. Law would allow them to stay if they sought asylum. These Human Exporters or smugglers are funded by the drug cartels who are working hand-in-hand with Middle East based terrorist organizations.[i] These smugglers are given specific orders to target families with young, sickly children. They promise them that once they are in the U.S. they will be given free medical care and reunited with any family members living in America. Although this may sound like a caring bunch of people, the fact is it has created the first wave of the invasion or attack on the United States by terrorists. This first wave is an attack using biological warfare with human beings as a platform of delivering diseases and illnesses.

The second phase of this planned terrorist invasion is the infiltration of "Jundi Allah" or "soldiers of god" for the purpose of bringing the fight of terrorism onto American soil.[ii] The chaos and confusion that the influx of illegal aliens has caused at every one of our border crossing sectors is being used as a smoke screen by these evil forces.

While our Customs and Border Patrol agents are busy taking care of families, these terrorists are crossing over by the dozens and disappearing into the population. They already have their fellow terrorists in America that have been living, training, and recruiting other radicals and ensuring all new arrivals have a place to live. The number of terrorists in America is growing and as they establish a stronger foothold in America, their goal of destroying us from within becomes a greater reality.

Abu Bakr al-Baghdadi, the leader of the militant Islamist group Islamic State in Iraq and the Levant (ISIL), now known as the Islamic State in Iraq and Syria (ISIS), warned America that he was "coming for us" according to congressional testimony in February 2014 from Deputy Assistant Secretary of State Brett McGurk. Al-Baghdadi has transformed a terrorist organization into a well equipped military force since his release from U.S. custody in 2009. This army is taking Iraq by force and looks to be moving forces farther south and west -- recruiting as they move. As ISIS moves farther into Iraq, these terrorists are taking over and exploiting sensitive ammunition warehouses and depots. In June 2014 ISIS has already taken over the chemical production plant in Samarra and latest reports show they now have short range ballistic missiles – SCUD Missiles to be exact.[iii] It is only a matter of time before they march in to Al-Taji and uncover the chemical warheads for the SCUD missiles. These warheads were the ones uncovered by my UNSCOM inspection team in 1998 that had been filled with SARIN Nerve Agent.

The goal of ISIS is simple: initially create an Islamic Caliphate in the Middle East with the Kingdom of Jordan as their next target, and once established, they will regroup, begin a stronger recruitment effort, and then move toward their ultimate goal: A world wide caliphate. They want to ensure the Islamic faith is the only recognized religion in the world.

Let me explain very quickly the analysis of what is happening along our border with Mexico. For the past two decades Border Patrol agents have routinely found evidence of OTM (Other Than Mexican) and OTCA (Other Than Central American) personnel crossing into the U.S.[iv] CBP evidence includes Arabic passports, Chinese identification cards, paperwork from Bosnia, Russia, Iran, and so many other nations. But the reports of the CBP agents have been ignored. Only Governor Jan Brewer of Arizona, Governor Susana Martinez of New Mexico, and Governor Rick Perry of Texas have had the intestinal fortitude to challenge the federal government on their lack of support to close off the border. And now the true state of the lack of border security is coming to the attention of the entire nation because the mass exodus from Central America and Mexico is affecting American's negatively.

But the reality is we have had border crossings for years and terrorists have always found ways to circumvent our security systems to enter the country and prepare for whatever orders they receive to disrupt the American way of life, or cause great numbers of casualties in the name of their Islamic beliefs. Terrorists cross into the U.S. through Mexico and Canada with ease. They are constantly learning from failed entry attempts and improving on the tactics they use in infiltrating the country of their biggest enemy. And those terrorists are coming here for the purpose of killing Americans and instilling their laws and beliefs into our society.

In the early part of 1996 intelligence reports indicated the moving of surface to air missiles into the U.S. via Canada along the East Coast. Sadly, FBI agents lost track of the missiles and coincidentally in July 1996 TWA-800 exploded in mid-air after taking off from John F. Kennedy International Airport.[v] Most witnesses to the accident had seen a "streak of light" that was unanimously described as ascending and moving to a point where a large fireball appeared, with several witnesses reporting that the fireball split in two as it descended toward the water. There was intense interest among the intelligence community top missile experts at the Defense Intelligence Agency and the Missile and Space Intelligence Center who went on record to say they could not rule out missile strike in this aircraft mishap.

This is just one incident. I could go on about the number of Hezbollah members we have stopped from entering the United States; or the number of al-Qaeda members that were detained upon their arrival into America but the bottom line is terrorists are here, they have an agenda, and they are hell-bent on destroying America.

How do I know this? No, this didn't come from the news. I am Biff Baxter and I have personally seen the eyes of terror. I have sat across the table from jihadists who wanted nothing more than to kill Christians in the name of Allah. In 1997 Saddam Hussein issued a death list where my name appeared in the 18th spot. I know terrorism and I tried hard to help stop it. But, unfortunately, my efforts were stopped by the very government that I served.

I was forced to retire in 1998 by the Clinton Administration who instituted a military draw-down to balance the budget (instead of cutting congressional money) and they froze my promotion to Master Sergeant. However, in the years that followed I was asked to work on different projects, one special project was to advise the leadership on new standard operating procedures to help improve Human Intelligence operations. I was tasked to provide independent analysis on terrorist related raw intelligence a few times, and finally, in 2003 I was asked to make one final trip to the Middle East on behalf of "a grateful nation that needs you", (or at least that is what the letter stated.)

In these past 3 years I have answered email's and phone calls from the same government agency I ended my career with, because they want to "get my take" on some reports. When told what the current administration was doing with my analysis and the current flow of terror related intelligence, I just shake my head with great disappointment at the arrogance portrayed by the President and his staff and I am saddened to see agencies like Defense Intelligence Agency, Central Intelligence Agency, and the Special Operations Command having to succumb to being politically correct.

Here is my bottom line: terrorism is evil and most terrorists are radicalized Muslims who have twisted minds and truly believe killing non-Muslims will get them to heaven.   Nothing more, nothing less. The Obama administration continues to tiptoe around this issue and now, too late, terrorism is coming to destroy America. Some even say he is part of the plan and when I try to defend the office of the President of the United States, those that argue with me point to Obama's own words in his autobiography: In Audacity of Hope he writes: "I will stand with the Muslims should the political winds shift in an ugly direction." The quote comes from page 261 of the paperback edition of The Audacity of Hope.[vi]

So in this book, Secrets Revealed – Terrorism, USA, I will dive into the dark place of terror in the United States. Not the homegrown knuckleheads who want to stop oil rigs from operating or trees from being cut down, but the terrorist movement that is borne of the hatred against America because it is a Christian nation. This march by Muslim based terrorists seeking to erase Christianity from the face of the earth while trampling on the Constitution of the United States as it is the main roadblock between their establishment of Sharia Law and our Freedom.

This is my story albeit some fiction added and names changed to protect the innocent and the classified. This story covers the period from the day I "unofficially" retired (October 1998) through the years I worked surreptitiously with the intelligence community (1998 – 2011), and my final assignment addressing terrorism that was ended abruptly by the Obama administration.

Buckle up… this gets bumpy.

Terrorism, U.S.A.

LOSS OF LIFE

My last official act while still in the military was working under assumed identity trying to retrieve information from a usually friendly country on a group of terrorists that were planning to conduct an attack against a significant embassy in Germany. I was working with the State Department in conjunction with agents from the CIA conducting an investigation on possible espionage activity within the embassy. Prior to that I was embedded with the United Nations as a Missile Inspector. Sending me on back-to-back missions was a stupid move because just a few months later I was sent back to Iraq supporting the State Department in the same capacity representing the Defense Intelligence Agency under my true name. So there I was in Baghdad living in the same hotel, seeing the same kids on the streets selling gum to UN Inspectors, but with a different name. Made no sense, but I just did what I had to do. My mission was to verify the location of the Sarin warheads my team had found during the earlier trip.

These were successful trips: Two embassy personnel were arrested and an espionage ring disrupted; not only did I verify the number of Sarin warheads in Iraq, but on my covert mission I was able to "tag" the twenty-seven warheads located in a warehouse in al-Taji Air Base and two "missing" launchers that subsequently ended up hidden in western Syria. I completed my UN obligations and headed home where I was greeted with the news that I was going into forced retirement, and my promotion to Master Sergeant would not go through. It was completely unexpected.

But life in the military is hard, and I was ready for the civilian life. The CIA had offered me a position as a desk officer, but there was no way I was going to work for those chuckleheads. And besides, I was tired of the Washington D.C. scene. I needed open areas with rolling hills and wildlife that wasn't behind bars and cages. So I packed up my belongings and moved to New Mexico. Why New Mexico? Because I could. And just when I was in the middle of my "see America" tour, I received a message alerting me that I was not "officially retired" from the Army yet. So now, instead of finding a place to live in northern New Mexico, I found myself on a plane heading back to Washington D.C.

After a good night sleep, thanks to a nightcap of chamomile tea with cardamom and some raspberry cookies, I woke up in a good mood and put on my uniform for hopefully the last time. Seeing I had some time to kill, I decided to visit some of the monuments that meant so much to me during my many years living in Alexandria. I made the obligatory stop at Arlington National Cemetery to pay my respects to my fallen brothers and sisters. I stood there in awe and watched the changing of the guard at the Tomb of the Unknown Soldier. I visited the Marine Corps Memorial, more commonly known as the Iwo Jima Memorial. After paying my respects, I looked at my wrist watch and realized I still had thirty minutes before the out-processing center would open. I walked over to the walking and biking path along the Potomac River and looked across the body of water; I was able to see the top of one of the many office complexes I worked from during my glory days. Many of the buildings located just off of Clarendon Boulevard in Arlington. As I stood there the emotion of the moment came over me, and I wept.

I was unaware of the little eyes that were gazing at me until I heard the voice of this little girl.

"Mommy, why is that man crying?"

I turned to see the little girl looking up to her mother for answers.

The mother immediately grabbed the girls hand and started to pull her away walking briskly toward a parking area as she told the little girl "come on, we don't need to be near people like that."

Wow! So that was it? My official last day in the Army, and I am considered a sub human that should be shunned. I was stunned, pulled off my beret and threw it into the Potomac. I don't know why I was surprised. There has been a growing lack of respect for our military in this country since the Vietnam era.

I walked back to my rental car and drove to Henderson Hall on Fort Myer. Finding a parking spot I again checked my watch and sat out the last five minutes of my career listening to some Lynyrd Skynyrd on a classic rock station pre-set in the Silver Grand Am. I entered Henderson Hall and followed the sign to an office with only one other soldier outside in the hallway waiting to go in. The door was opened and the other soldier and I signed in for, (what better be) the last time. The clerk called me after about ten minutes and after verifying my social security number I was sent to the Out Processing Clerk for the Military District, Washington D.C.

Choosing not to sit, I stood in front of the desk of an administrator who could have been a member of a hip-hop boy band. Specialist Fourth Class Chapman grabbed my files and immediately started to feverishly type forms completing my time in service and updating entries on the part of my personnel record known as the DA Form 2-1. The DA Form 2-1 was something all soldiers were familiar with because it was the document promotion boards would look at to determine whether or not the soldier would move up in the ranks. Sort of a quick-look at assignments, schools, medals and awards.

He looked at one of the papers in the file, looked at me curiously, and then looked back down and shook his head.

"Sir" the specialist kept his eyes on a form that was covered with a 'For Official Use Only' cover. "Are you sure you are supposed to be here?"

I looked at the young man not sure what to make of this question. "Well specialist, I just finished my last assignment and this is where I was told to report so that I can officially retire."

Chapman picked up the phone and pressed four numbers. "Morning sir. I am sorry to bother you…, yes sir I…, no sir but…"

The kid was getting a first class butt chewing over the phone. I also took his body language as indifferent to the conversation since it was evident he was ready to spring something that would shut the mouth of the moron on the other end of the phone conversation.

"Yes sir… SIR!" Specialist Chapman had had enough. "I have a Victor Four, Sierra One down here trying to retire. And he's on the AWOL list."

"AWOL? Absent without Leave? What is going on?" I thought to myself.

Chapman leaned back in his chair and held the handset away from his ear allowing me to hear the other person.

"I'll be right there. Thank you specialist. Good work."

Chapman hung up the phone as a sergeant came over from another desk. "Dude you so got him. That was awesome." The sergeant looked at me and extended his hand. "Sir, I am Sergeant Aranda. Thank you for your service. We will have this all figured out in just a little bit. Chapman and I will make sure every form is perfect."

"Well, thank you guys, but please explain to me what the heck is going on? I'm not AWOL and what is a Victor four?"

I was a bit confused having never had a negative mark in my record. Well except for that time I inadvertently destroyed classified documents... and a safe... and an armored personnel carrier... but it was "an accident."

Well I might as well explain.

Flashback: I was a private first class and no one had ever explained to me that when we did drills or alerts, they were just practice to see if we understood the steps to take in case war broke out and we had to actually deploy to the war zone. I was stationed in Bamberg, Germany and we had been placed on alert. I drove the M-577 (armored personnel carrier and mobile command post) to the front of the command headquarters for 3rd Brigade, 1st Armored Division. Once there my NCO's had arrived and started to load the M-577 while I was sent to the motor pool to bring up the other section vehicles. It seems the Intelligence Officers jeep-driver was too lazy to do it and the driver of the Gamma-Goat (a six-wheel drive monster) lived off base and it would take him a while to get to the base.

I ran to the motor-pool, a quick half mile, and brought the jeep with its trailer. The Intelligence Officer (or S-2) was there, smiled and thanked me, and asked where his driver was. "Still sleeping sir; sorry, gotta go get the Goat."

Inside I was laughing because I knew I just got his driver in trouble which was okay with me because he got preferential treatment. As I trotted off I heard the S-2 holler to the NCO in charge "Sergeant Jennings! Why the hell is private Baxter doing all the work again?"

The word 'again' fired me up. Not sure why some people in the army didn't pull their weight, but if you join the Army you better be ready for a 24 hour a day, seven day a week lifestyle… in other words, NO WIMPS!

So I made it into the Gamma-Goat and started out the motor pool when the ugliest sound in the world brought the Goat to a halt. I miss-shifted and actually dropped the drive shaft. Oh shoot! I ran back to the HQ and reported it to one of the section sergeants.

We finished packing the M-577 and the Jeep and when we received the word over the radio to move out for maneuvers, we convoyed with the rest of the staff elements to our ready area in accordance with our General Defense Plan (GDP). We backed in four M-577's, pulled out their extensions and in a matter of thirty minutes we had our field command post. I was placed on night shift and the Operations NCO S-3 Section (who was a complete jerk) decided he would have fun with the privates who were stuck on the night shift.

The S-3 sergeant received an "Exercise" message that the Soviet forces had crossed the border and were advancing through the Fulda Gap. He ran to the S-1/4 M-577 (Admin/Supply) and the Fire Support M-577 and delivered the message. When he came to my area he was animated and scared.

"Private Baxter, we are being overrun. I am sending my specialist to wake up the command staff. I need you to put your emergency evacuation plan in motion. Got it?!"

I looked at him confused. "Sergeant, where do I find that?"

"Dang it private! In your field SOP! Go! Go! Go!"

I found the Standard Operating Procedures and looked through the tabs… emergency evacuation. I quickly scanned the document. Holy smokes, this was the real deal! We were in war. My adrenaline was high and I just wanted to make sure my every action was 'by the book'.

"Sergeant," I hollered to the S-3 side of the Command Post (CP) "has the command element been alerted."

"Yes!"

I looked around to see all the personnel in the CP busy and walking back and forth.

I checked off the list. Staff alerted – check. Classified documents placed in field safe – check. Maps and overlays erased – check. Radio frequency booklet placed in field safe – check. I was getting through the list and proud that my bosses would come in to the CP in a few moments and congratulate me.

I sat down after grabbing a Pepsi out of the section cooler that was strapped to the top of the M-577.

"What the hell are you doing Baxter?" the S-3 sergeant was mad! "Is your checklist complete?"

"No sergeant, I was waiting on sergeant Jennings."

"We do not have time to wait. Get the list complete. You can sit down when it is done." He stormed away.

I grabbed the list and went over everything I had completed. Just one step left. I put on my flak vest, helmet, and grabbed my rifle. Looked around and put the final step into action.

I grabbed the Thermite Grenade and pulled the pin placing the grenade on top of the field safe. I ran out of the M-577 and hollered "Fire in the hole."

A powerful incendiary device, thermite grenades produce intense heat through a chemical reaction. Thermite is known as a "pyrotechnic composition" that burns intensely when ignited. When detonated, some thermite grenades have been known to burn at temperatures of up to 4,000 degrees Fahrenheit. The extreme heat makes thermite grenades good for destroying weapons caches, bunkers, vehicles and in this case, the field safe and all the classified documents and radio frequency instructions known as the CEOI.

Thankfully, at the hearing it was determined that the S-3 NCO, who had pulled a prank on me, was found to be responsible for the unlawful destruction of classified material and the subsequent destruction of government property as we also found out the thermite grenades are capable of burning through a field safe and the hull of an M-577 armored personnel carrier in seconds. *End of Flashback.*

"Sergeant Baxter, they had you listed as AWOL. This is not uncommon for those in your specialty. Now your additional skill identifiers are S-1 and V-4 which means you were an advanced source handler or basically a super secret HUMINT guy. Normally we can't handle your retirement here, but instead of sending you to Fort Meade, we can make sure you are taken care of here. That's also why Chapman called the colonel. He's going to administer a debrief oath and have you sign some forms." Aranda pointed to some seats near his desk.

"There is some fresh coffee over by my desk. Not Folgers or any stuff like that, but I like it."

"What kind of coffee is it?" My curiosity was piqued so I made my way to the coffee carafe.

"It's a blend of sorts. A little Yemen, a little Indonesian." He smiled.

"Is it Mocca Java?" The look on his face was awesome.

"Yes! A man who knows his coffee." He walked to his desk and opened up a drawer and pulled out a coffee mug that was wrapped in plastic.

"Here," he handed me the cup after unwrapping it. "A man who knows his coffee does not drink from Styrofoam in my presence."

I poured myself a cup and sat down to enjoy the offerings of my new friend. As I enjoyed the coffee I looked around at the typical Army office: Posters of Operations Security; Subversion and Espionage Directed against the Army (SAEDA), and the obligatory photographs of the chain of command.

The coffee was taking me to a relaxing place in my mind. Mocca Java is a natural combination of Yemen coffee that Dutch mercantile ships picked up on their trade route running through the port city of Mocca and the java they loaded on board in Djakarta. The two coffees are a perfect match; the light, tangy coffee of Yemen is balanced by full, sweet coffee of Java. This was an incredible blend and was a great way to finalize my career in the Army.

Aranda and Chapman were going back and forth to a locked cabinet in the back of the office pulling out different forms. Clearly they knew what they were doing, but what was also clear was this HUMINT retiring thing was not something that happened often.

I sat there just daydreaming. My career was full and complete to say the least. But clearly, the last five years were the most hectic and caused me the most physical; and if I were completely honest, psychological damage. My back was constantly killing me; my migraines were a weekly gift from the pain world; and my numb left leg was a great test on muscle memory, because quite simply, it's tough to walk when you can't feel your leg (the price you pay when you fall out of a helicopter).

But the late night whispers of people from my past and the vivid dreams of missions I was a part of created the greatest scar that I carry. I frequently find myself up at 2 AM looking out the windows or patrolling the hallway. I need to find the off switch to my mind so I can be a normal human being.

I kicked my head back and closed my eyes. Oh if only I were on a beach somewhere. Yes, a nice beach…

"Sergeant Baxter… sergeant… BIFF!"

I jumped as my daydream was interrupted. Of course years of training and incredible physical prowess allowed me to react without spilling a drop of coffee.

"Is everything okay sergeant?" a colonel stood in front of me as I was gathering my thoughts.

"Well sir, things were going great until I was brought out of my daydream. I guess I will never know how great a dancer Cher is." The colonel showed a hint of a smile.

"Well sergeant, I am Colonel Sanders." He stood there and I think he was expecting a salute or something.

"Oh nice. Didn't recognize you without your white suit or beard." I extended my hand for a handshake but instead found that this colonel was not in the mood for humor.

"You are still in the military Sergeant, and I am not a man of levity. As a matter of fact, I am not a man that is happy in his current assignment. I am an Air Defender, and I need to be with air defenders."

His stern tone was a sign of a man who was one step away from snapping.

Aranda and Chapman, meanwhile, stood behind the Colonel and were silently cracking up and clearly loving the moment.

"No disrespect intended sir." I again extended my hand "I am grateful for your service and actually glad to have a combat arms colonel here for my final day. Makes it feel official."

Oh yes, I was the king of surreptitious sucking up. It was a ploy I used in the HUMINT world to turn many people into assets. You take one of their weaknesses and swing it to your advantage.

He grabbed my hand and shook it purposefully.

"Thank you sergeant. I am glad to be here for you."

Most of the time, an officer assigned to work with Air Defense Artillery (Air Defender) either graduated very low in his class or was a glutton for punishment. Some would classify the ADA soldier as a trained monkey, but not me. I respect all our fellow soldiers – simian or not. So working an Air Defender with my HUMINT mind tricks was like spreading butter on bread. Easy because they tend to be stiff like stale bread and all you have to do is know how to work the knife.

"Sergeant Aranda, you and Specialist Chapman join us in the conference room. Bring Sergeant Baxter's files and the debriefing box." Sanders turned and signaled me to follow him.

"Oh yes," he turned abruptly and I almost ran into him, "Sergeant Aranda, check the Special Access Program database for any additional instructions on Baxter."

We walked into a conference room where I was directed to sit in a chair near the door.

"Sir, can I sit somewhere else. I am uncomfortable not facing the door."

"Oh, yes, sure. Occupational hazard I assume." He chuckled "You know sergeant, I envy you."

"Sir, I know this goes against your nature but can you please just call be Biff?"

"Sure thing Biff. I'm Terry. But, I am sure you understand in front of my men…"

"No problem sir. Now you were saying you envy me. How is that?"

"You are retiring. I want to retire. I have twenty-two years in and I can pull the plug whenever I want, but I just want one more shot with a maneuver unit. I don't even care what my role is… I want to go out as a warrior. I don't know if that makes sense to you."

"It makes plenty of sense Colonel. I still feel like I have one more mission left in me. But, I guess it is time to go." I looked at Sanders and saw he truly was a man who was desperately wanting to have that 'one last shot'.

Just as the silence had become awkward Aranda and Chapman walked in with a handful of files. Chapman sat next to me and placed a folder in front of me while Aranda walked over to Sanders and whispered into his ear and then sat next to the colonel with the other files. Sanders opened one of the files and placed a loose paper Aranda had also been carrying in the file marked "*Official Documents – Do Not Release*".

"Biff, what are you feeling right now?" Sanders looked at me as he asked the question while Aranda and Chapman looked stunned at the colonels' use of my first name.

I looked at the colonel and then to Aranda. I glanced at Chapman and smiled as I saw a young man who had a many years ahead of him. I returned my stare to the now empty cup of coffee and focused on the drop or two at the bottom.

"I feel loss…" I started, and I reached my finger into the cup and touched the coffee drops. I stared at my finger and the beautiful color of the coffee and continued.

"It is a loss of life. The army is what I have known since I left high school. I grew up in the army. I lived army. I breathed army and I almost died army… three times." I chuckled and then licked the coffee off of my finger.

"Colonel," I wiped my finger on my pant leg and looked at Sanders "I am not ready for today."

"Well then the feeling is mutual. Looks like the army is not ready for today either. Sergeant Aranda pulled this message on the SAP database. It is from the PERSCOM message center." Sanders passed it across the table where I eagerly grabbed it to read its contents.

"Seems the army may have one last mission for you." Sanders voice was a bit shaky.

The message came through the Personnel Command but originated from CENTCOM (Central Command) based out of MacDill Air Force Base. It was marked For Official Use Only/Sensitive and outlined a follow on mission to some of the work I had begun with Task Force Dragon Fire. Counter Terrorism stuff. But this time it was an AO (Area of Operation) I was not familiar with, the AO was the United States.

"Sir, this says I would have to extend for three years and that I would have to call the operations center."

"Phones right here and we can leave the room if you need privacy."

"Thank you sir. Can I have just ten minutes?"

"Let's go, gentlemen." Sanders got up and took Aranda and Chapman with him. I dialed the number listed on the message.

"Central Command Task Force Dragon Fire, this line is not secured, how may I help you?"

"Hi, this is Sergeant First Class Baxter. I am calling reference orders number 042A-0012 can you direct me to the right person?"

"This is the right person, Biff. Are you ready to get back to work?"

SECRETS REVEALED:

ONE LAST SHOT

I will always place the mission first.
I will never accept defeat.
I will never quit.
I will never leave a fallen comrade.

The Warrior Ethos is something good leaders try to instill in their soldiers. But the bottom line is this 'way of life' is in our DNA. Either you have it or you don't. I lived the Warrior Ethos and most of the guys I trained and served with did the same. Meeting Colonel Terry Sanders also reinforced in me that there are those who still have that "one last mission" attitude and all they want is to be a part of one more adrenaline rush before considering their career complete. Those that don't get that opportunity are the ones who sit around telling stories all day long. And the older they get, the greater the stories were. And so being compassionate of this condition, I requested the good colonel be allowed to join me in this final mission after my phone conversation with CENTCOM.

Despite the fact that there was a Top Secret communiqué that had come out detailing a hit-list developed by the dictator of Iraq, and that I was on that list, I still felt that if I had to go into that country I would be okay. The Dictator of Iraq had issued a death list of twenty-five Americans in 1997 or 1998 which included "yours truly" coming in at an impressive eighteen.

What is very disturbing is that one would think I was safe on American soil.[vii] Analysts with connection to Task Force Dragon Fire had begun an investigation that revealed the infiltration of America and, even more troubling, the intelligence world, by terrorist cells. This is a disheartening picture of our national security in the United States, and for the most part, the security of nations around the world. Many splinter cells were popping up throughout the United States and the western hemisphere under the guise of sympathizers in support of the cry for compassion by radical Islamic terrorists posing as legitimate businesses or religious organizations.

But needless to say, terrorism is not new. On any given day we can be assured that there are people coming into the United States with the sole intent of killing Americans or disrupting the American way of life. Anyone associated with America is a target too. Why? That is the troubling part, we just can't pinpoint any reason other than hate. They hate us! And equally troubling is that on any given day we can also be assured that there are people leaving the United States to either report intelligence to terrorist headquarters or travel to foreign training camps to join the Jihad against the West.

As baffling as this may sound, there is no true religious connection that condones the actions of these radicals. Their financiers are mostly gullible billionaires who have bought into the faux cry for justice by these terrorists. They blindly give their money to these businesses with promises that their money was going to a worthy cause while also believing they will never be found out. In return, the terrorist organization promises them either more business or protection from the violence occurring in the countries that their businesses are located. But what they do not realize is no one can hide. NSA has tabs on most all donors and has even tracked money used by terrorists to major corporations based in the United States.

Can this activity be stopped? One of my last missions with the military involved combating a former intelligence asset who turned to terrorism because the money was so good. It was money that bought off Uwe Cuvellier and his thugs allowing them to maintain a multi-million dollar company that was "supposed" to be joining in the fight against terrorism. All the while they were merely creating a smoke screen to cover their own terrorist activities. It was money, we later found out, which turned Caterina Montes, a member of the State Department working in Panama, into a modern day Mata-Hari that was in charge of the backup plan to have me killed. The sad part? She was planning my demise and other terrorist activities with a rogue CIA Agent, Tina Ferguson, also lured into the fold by promises of millions of dollars and safe passage to the country of her choice where she could hide without fear of extradition.

Yes, America has been infiltrated by terrorists and reinforcements arrive every day. Hamas and Hezbollah operatives are being smuggled into the United States daily across the porous U.S./Mexico border. And as hard as our Border Patrol Agents work, there are not enough of them to cover the vast frontier that stretches from San Diego, California to just east of McAllen, Texas. Over 1,500 miles of border area and that is just to our south.

So now I sit in a conference room in Fort Myer with Colonel Terry Sanders, waiting for another phone call where the two of us will be briefed on the new mission addressing terrorism in the U.S.

The phone rang and Sanders answered and initiated the keying requirements allowing us to speak on a classified level over this special phone.

"So Biff, how the hell are you my friend?" It was Bernie Griffin, a gentlemen from the CIA I had worked with on my last mission. His tone was jovial yet businesslike.

"I'm doing okay. But now I am curious as to what your connection is with CENTCOM."

"No problem Biff, we are working with CENTCOM on a serious situation. I know you had helped establish Dragon Fire and we wanted to get you in on this latest development. But I want to know what your plans are, what is next for Biff Baxter?"

"Well, I really haven't thought about it. I am just taking it one day at a time and when the colonel here handed me the orders I had to check it out. But I still want to take a vacation and sort things out." I locked my hands behind my head and leaned back in the office chair to stretch.

"Well, let me toss these options at you."

"Just to make it clear Bernie, I'm not working for the CIA." I just looked up at the ceiling maintaining my stretching position.

"Wait, Biff, hear me out. Option one: work for the agency as an analyst or consultant to this Dragon Fire effort. No travel, just desk work."

I was shaking my head no as he continued his sales pitch even though I knew he couldn't see me.

"Not interested Bernie."

"Okay, Option two, you come instruct at the academy or the farm." He paused for a reaction but I continued to shake my head.

"Try again; and remember, I have a distinguished colonel sitting with me that I want as part of the team, this had better be good." I smiled and winked at Sanders. He just sat there with a look of disbelief.

"Okay Biff, then how about this…"

I stopped him before he could continue his sentence. "And remember, Bernie, I am not going to work for the CIA or any other Intelligence Agency."

"I got it Biff. Now I know today is the day you officially retire from the military and you get your nice eleven hundred dollars a month, and you don't need money. And you can live quietly forever knowing that you did the best you could while serving. But can we just ask one more mission from you?"

"Bernie, the Army is the one that told me it was time to retire. I would love to stay, but just cut to the chase and tell me what this is all about."

"Well, I know you remember Uwe and, oh by the way there is another hefty reward check waiting for you. But we are finding out that Uwe is just the tip of the iceberg. Terrorist organizations have infiltrated the intelligence community, the military, and some analysts believe they have even infiltrated our political leaders. We want you and a team of your choosing to break the code on how they are coming in and how they are being financed."

I grabbed a pen from the table and scribbled a note to Sanders – it read: Don't laugh, I am about to frustrate him.

"So Bernie, how much is the reward check for?"

"Really Biff?"

"Yeah, how much and when can I get it?"

"I can get it to you today. But what about the mission?"

"How much is it for Bernie? I wanted to take the colonel to dinner tonight to thank him…"

"Dammit Biff, you're a jerk. The check is for one-hundred fifty thousand. I will personally bring it to you if you want. But what about the mission? Can I count you in?"

"Do I have to wait to cash it?"

"No Biff, the CIA is good for it."

"I don't know Bernie, I am hearing some troubling reports out of the CIA."

"Biff!" the voice was tired but you can tell he was finally catching on as he chuckled. "Come on man. Are you in? We really need you."

"Bernie, yes. Under one condition."

"What is that Biff?"

"I want you to say 'Biff is my big daddy and I am just a wannabe'."

"Really Biff?" I could almost see him face palming.

"Colonel do you really want to be in charge of this clown?"

Sanders looked at the phone as if to force the stern look through the wires. "Not a chance Bernie. He will be in charge of me."

I reached across the table and shook his hand. "Welcome aboard" I whispered.

"Great." Bernie sounded relieved. "Gentlemen I have booked you both on a plane to Dallas. Don't ask questions, we will meet there. Too many listening devices up there in the D.C. area. I know Dallas brings back bad memories Biff, but it's the safest place right now."

"Roger, Bernie. Hey, I have thought it over. I am going to complete the retirement process today and you can put me on the consultation contract if that is okay with you."

"That's great Biff. I will send the forms so you can have them filled out when we meet up in Dallas."

"Great, when do we leave?" I looked at Sanders and gestured to see if that was okay with him. He looked absolutely excited. I swear this news made him look ten years younger.

"As soon as you guys get to Dulles give the United Airlines check in clerk your names and tell them it is agency business. They'll call us and we verify that you are with us; the tickets are ready for you now. I am leaving Tampa to meet you both there."

"Okay Bernie, we'll see you there."

We disconnected the phone and Sanders looked at me. "Is this for real?"

"Yes sir, this is how my entire career went."

"What did he mean when he said Dallas would bring back bad memories?"

"It was my last mission. Bernie and I worked together. I had to take down a good friend. He just fell into the wrong group of people. But I don't really want to talk about it. It was also a time I thought I was already retired." I laughed and so did Sanders.

"Well what do we do now Biff?"

"Well Terry. We head to Dallas."

We walked out of the conference room and Sanders called out to Aranda and Chapman.

"Gentlemen, I am sorry if I was a jerk. I just did not want to be here. But starting today, I am out of your hair. I don't know what else to tell you but, thanks and good luck."

34

Sanders really didn't know how to handle this situation.

"Sir, good luck to you. And by the way, we got this fax a few seconds ago. We kind of knew you were leaving." Aranda handed him the fax which was a copy of orders assigning him immediately to the commander, Central Command.

"Wow. These friends of yours are good." Sanders held out the papers to show me his orders.

"Sir," Chapman chimed in "if you need anything, just remember there are some desk jockeys here that would really like to get out and do something for their country."

I saluted the two of them and walked away. Sanders followed suit and we walked to my rental car.

"Biff, what do I do with my car?"

"It's safe here. We will need it when we get back." I really didn't know what to tell him but that seemed like the most logical answer.

"Well," Sanders got into my rental car. "I wanted adventure…"

He was smiling as we drove off towards the International Airport in Dulles.

Terrorism, U.S.A.

SABBATICAL

Bernie met us in Dallas and told me he wanted an anti-terrorism team formed up in a month or so. He would take care of the omnipresent bureaucratic garbage that came with setting up a special access program. Especially a program that, for all intents and purposes, should fall under the auspices of a black or covert program. Sanders immediately signed up since clearly this was the "last hurrah" he had been looking for. I was not so gung-ho. I needed my rest and some time to clear my mind so after talking to Bernie and Sanders; I headed back to New Mexico to finish off what I had started – getting my new home in order. Of course I was warned to keep my phone nearby. I was soon back in the mode of rest and relaxation while contemplating my next move with the military and the agency.

It was strange waking up in the mornings with no real schedule or agenda bogging me down. Sadly my mind and body were still used to waking up at an unthinkable hour. So I took advantage of the early morning conundrum and prepared coffee in my French press then walk out to the front porch of my new home near Raton, New Mexico. The sunrise was always majestic, and I enjoyed the cool mornings. There was an absolute peace in this part of the nation. Looking across the fields towards the beautiful mountains and the occasional deer grazing in my front yard. I couldn't have picked a better place to clear my mind... without medication. I sipped my coffee remembering how I actually decided on settling in Raton.

Another Flashback: It was after my final mission with the U.S. Army where I had helped bring down a dangerous terror support group that had infiltrated the government system. The CIA was running the show and after it was all said and done they presented me an unexpected gift. A red Corvette. Now this was not your run of the mill corvette that anyone can walk into the car dealership and purchase. No, this was a government test vehicle that I just happened to help transport across the country for the Technical Support Working Group and their chief, General Raney and his detection team. Of course, they had it stripped down of most of the "gee whiz" nuclear, biological and chemical detection sensors but left the onboard computers and, of course, the killer Blaupunkt sound system. And since it was after all, a corvette, it was a great ride. So after being presented the keys and thinking my time in the military was officially over, I took a leisurely drive to Albuquerque and spent the night relaxing at the Marriott Pyramid. In the morning I completed my journey heading north on I-25 for about four hours until I arrived at the Raton city limits.

I checked the onboard computer and contacted a real estate agent who actually agreed to meet with me at the Arby's. I was hungry but I really wanted to look at houses immediately. I thought about calling my good friend, Gary and his bride, but then again, I wanted to surprise them in the morning. I took a seat at the Arby's and settled in to their 5 for $5 special and a bucket of iced tea.

A young lady approached me and introduced herself as Ms. Pamela Ninneman owner of Home Associates in Raton. She sat down and after listening to my small list of "must-haves" she turned her laptop to show me a few listings she would "love to take you to…"

There were your obligatory golf-course homes, a few trailers on the outskirts of town and many "handyman" specials. But when it was all said and done, I settled for a four-bedroom ranch-style with a finished basement that was set against the mountains leading to Sugarite Canyon. The master bedroom had French doors that led out to a wrap-around porch. It was the perfect place for my morning coffee and quiet time with the Creator while overlooking the beautiful view of Sugarite Canyon to my north and a valley to the northwest looking towards the Colorado border. The key was the peaceful surroundings and so, to seal the deal, I played no games; I offered them cash. No stress of house payments with the sole intent of securing this oasis with no noise pollution from society.

I went into town to look for things to make my new house more like a home. I gave a call to my good friend Gary but once again he and his bride were on another cruise and wouldn't be back for another two weeks. So I asked Ms. Ninneman for any recommendations and she gave me the names of a few locals that were good at interior decorating. I visited some of them but really wasn't willing to give up all designing control to just anyone. That was until I met up with a young lady who not only was extremely beautiful and pleasant, but had an interesting name: Prudencia Sarkisian. Prudencia was an incredibly intelligent woman with looks to match. She was five foot five with an athletic build. Her legs gave her away as a runner. Her brown hair perfectly combed with well maintained eyebrows, pleasant light application of makeup, and an incredible smile. Her eyes glistened and instantly made me feel at ease. There was no threat here, only beauty, inside-out.

Ms Sarkisian and I checked our calendars and settled on meeting in two weeks while she finished off another design she was working on at a hotel in Cimarron. So, in the interim, I promised myself I was not going to fall into the trap of vegetating in front of a television and scouted the area for other distracters. I occasionally went into Raton to check my post office box and pick up some provisions. I would head over to the Raton Range and pick up a few newspapers that I would read and then save for kindling for the roaring fires I was planning to have in the winter. I had earlier picked up a four-wheeler at the Honda dealership and went out on nature rides. One of my favorite rides crossed over into Colorado near Walton Lake. I found an old cabin near San Miguel Canyon that I marked on my map as a place to use should the weather ever turn bad while I was out and about.

I was enjoying my life of solitude. With plans of hunting and fishing every now and then with my old friends and some new ones I was ready to do some serious R & R.

Unfortunately my rest and relaxation was interrupted with an urgent message delivered by the U.S. Postal Service from the Commander, Military District, Washington, D.C. It seems I was not completely retired from the Army and they were, in essence, recalling me to finish out processing. I called my friend Gary and let him know I was going to be gone for a few days. I also called the interior decorator and moved the appointment to a later date. She was very accommodating. *End of Flashback*.

While I pressed restart on my Raton life, Bernie had taken Sanders back to the beltway to start working on the new anti-terrorism effort and I was allowed to take some much needed rest and relaxation in my new hometown. I was ready to pick up where I had left off. I would continue working on establishing my home and enjoy my life. Or at least the part of my life I would be able to enjoy until Bernie came calling.

I called the interior decorator, Prudencia Sarkisian and she agreed to meet me at the house. I had prepared some coffee and served it with some homemade almond biscotti wedges. We discussed my household needs and as I spoke she sat there soaking it all in, taking notes and occasionally smiled and nodded in affirmation of what I just described. We took a little tour of the house and I pointed out a few of the features I liked and those I hated, like the pink toilet and tub. When we returned to the sitting room I freshened the coffee and sat down to await her prognosis.

"Well Ms. Sarkisian, can she be fixed?" I smiled and sat back in my fold out chair that was better suited for a card table in a garage.

"Mr. Baxter you have impressed me."

"And how is that?"

I smiled as I took a sip of my Sumatran Reserve coffee I had ordered from Gevalia.

"You are the first man that has not wanted his home designed around a television and surround-sound system." She opened up a laptop computer and started tapping away at the keys.

"Well, I am not into television. I get my stimulation from Mother Nature. And can you please just call me

Biff?" I was trying to sound cool but then realized, I didn't need to sound cool... I wake up in a state of coolness.

"Okay Biff, this is what I would like to do for you." She got up and brought her laptop to me and sat in the folding chair next to me.

I looked at the modest design and noticed there was going to be some demolition and reconstruction needed to meet my desires for a gourmet kitchen and half-way decent bathroom.

"How long do you think this will take?" I grabbed the laptop to zoom in on the kitchen area.

"Well if you are going to pitch in and do some of the work, we can finish in about one week. If not, this may take me two weeks." She took the computer and started to walk to the kitchen.

"This kitchen will take the majority of the effort to incorporate the outside grilling area with the indoor area and it will require some building permits."

I got up to follow Prudencia to the kitchen when the inevitable happened. My phone rang.

I looked. It was Bernie. He never did have good timing.

"I have to take this," I said.

I walked back to the great room as she pulled out a measuring tape and started to measure walls and counters in the kitchen.

I hesitantly answered the phone.

"This is Biff"

"Biff! This is Bernie. How are things going?"

"Not bad Bernie. I actually have an interior designer here looking at sprucing up the place." I looked over to see Prudencia looking under the sink. I was a bit embarrassed that I kind of was ogling her. I was never the kind to ogle.

"Great! So you bought a place or are you renting?"

"I bought it," I said.

I was starting to sense the niceties before the trap-door so I rushed him along. "So what gives Bernie, I know you aren't calling me about my new home."

"Well Biff, you are partially correct. But since you asked I want to make an offer or maybe as you might call it, a twist to our existing deal." He paused. "How about I send a team out there and we secure a room for you. You know, give you a home SCIF. That way you can work from home and keep prying eyes away from our operation. And to sweeten the deal, you never really have to travel."

"Wait." I responded with a hint of annoyance.

"You want to add a Sensitive Compartmented Information Facility to my home?"

I was now whispering and walking to the opposite side of the house so that Prudencia wouldn't hear what Bernie was proposing.

"Bernie, I've got a basement and all I am going to do is store my firearms safes in there."

"We can give you an arms room too." Bernie laughed. "How you sitting for ammo? We can bring some of that out to you too."

"Bernie, are you talking about making my home a safe house for the agency?"

"Well, damn Biff that is a great idea. If you want, we can get a team out there in the next couple of weeks to start the work."

"You're an idiot Bernie. It was your idea. But yeah. Why don't you come out in three weeks. I will be working with my interior decorator to finish things up and then we can get the SCIF out of the way."

"Is she good looking Biff?"

"How do you know it's a she Bernie?"

"Because you ARE Biff Baxter." Again he laughed. "Hey give me her name and we'll run a check on her."

"No thanks Bernie. When can I expect you?"

"How about we figure one month from today. Good with you?" He said.

"Yeah I guess." I was hesitant. Something was amiss.

"Okay great. I'll talk with you as we get closer."

"Okay Bernie. We'll talk at you later."

"Hey Biff wait." And there it was. I knew there was something more.

"What's up Bernie?"

"I shipped off some reading material for you. It should get there today. It's some stuff on old Dragon Fire topics. Sanders is working out great but I need your take on this information."

"I'll read it when I get to it. Won't check the mail for another day or two."

"No worries, it's being delivered to your home."

"And I take it you already have my physical address? I figured as much Bernie. See you in a month."

"Okay Biff. Take care. Oh and per our agreement," he said sarcastically. "I am paying you for your help. Enjoy." He hung up and I stayed on a few seconds.

Click click click

I had to make sure his automatic encryption device disconnected otherwise my phone would still be in a secure mode and I wouldn't be able to call anyone until I called him again, reestablish the link, and terminated the scrambler.

I walked back to the kitchen where Prudencia was still tapping away at her keyboard.

44

"Sorry about that. How does it look? Will you be able to give me the gourmet kitchen of my dreams?"

"Yes I will Biff." She closed up her laptop. "But the bad news is it will not be cheap."

"Hold on." I opened up my phone, texted my bank for a balance.

"I don't have a problem with cost... I just got paid."

To say the CIA was thorough would be an understatement. No sooner did I tell Bernie I would read through the information he was having delivered that they deposited $18.5k in my account.

Prudencia looked at me and smiled.

"Good, because I already know where to order the appliances and building material and I sent them an email telling them what I was going to need. I also have a team that will be here in the morning to start demolition, my cousin will bring the building permits with him."

"Wow. That is quick. So do we need to do anything now?"

"No sir. We can start first thing in the morning."

"Well, then, how about dinner? Can I take you out to dinner or do you need to go home to your family?"

"I am not married Biff. Dinner would be fine." She looked at her watch. "It's only 2:30 though."

"Would you believe dinner in Colorado Springs? I know a great pizza place." Just the thought of a pizza from Fargo's Pizza Company was enough to send me into culinary convulsions of happiness.

"Well, then, let's go." Prudencia said with a smile.

"Really?... I mean, great!"

I grabbed my wallet off the kitchen counter and we walked outside to the driveway. With chivalry still alive and well I opened the passenger door of the Corvette for

Prudencia. She got in and immediately looked around the interior with great astonishment.

"What is all this?"

I started the car, hit a few buttons and turned on the onboard computer system.

"It's like GPS only fancier." I pressed the voice command button. "Fargo's Pizza in Colorado Springs please." The computer pulled up a map on the heads up display of the car while displaying a menu on the passenger side sun visor.

"Fargo's Pizza Biff. One Hundred Forty Nine Miles. Roughly two hours. Be careful for possible speed trap once you get off the Raton Pass."

"Oh my gosh this is awesome! Is this really your car? It's like that talking car show that was on the television years ago." Prudencia was clearly impressed.

"No, this is much better and I am better looking than that Hasselhof fella." I laughed.

I pulled out of the drive and made my way towards the highway. Once off the side roads I headed north on I-25 to Colorado Springs. Prudencia was still looking around the car and pressing different buttons. She was amazed that there was a computer display on her sun-visor and even more impressed when I opened the glove compartment to expose a keyboard. She navigated the internet courtesy of the satellite uplink and then clicked on my icon for Slacker Radio.

"Will this work in the car?" she asked in utter amazement.

"Yes ma'am. It is a satellite link. I have internet anywhere I go."

"Impressive." She clicked on the Slacker Radio Icon and tuned into my Jean Luc Ponty station, adjusting the volume to a pleasant background music level.

"So Biff," she started as she stored the keyboard and crossed her incredibly beautiful athletic legs. "Why did you move to Raton?"

"Well," I hesitated as I made sure to keep my eyes on the road. "I have friends that live here so I visited a few times and even spent a weekend or two at the NRA Whittington Center. I guess you can say this place kinda grew on me."

"That's it? You moved here "just because"? How about a girlfriend?" I could feel her eyes staring at me as she asked the questions.

"Well, to be honest, there was a cutie that used to sell corn dogs at the race track. I thought I would go visit just in case, but now that the track is closed I guess that idea is out the betting window."

"La Mesa Park? You used to go to La Mesa Park Horse Racing track?"

"Yeah, a long time ago." Her piercing stare was starting to freak me out.

"Oh my gosh" she started laughing hysterically. "Did you ever tip the concession stand girl twenty dollars and tell her she should be in the movies?"

I swerved the car as I turned my head to get another look at Ms. Sarkisian who was laughing so hard she was almost in tears. I neared the Raton Pass Port of Entry and pulled over to make sense of this revelation.

"How do you know about that?" I stared and realized her face was familiar but the eyes were not what I remembered.

"That was me." She was still laughing and blushing. "My sisters and I worked at the track. We used to call you the 'handsome stranger'."

"Uhm… now I am confused; actually I am blown away right now." I pulled into a parking spot and placed the car in park and turned to face her. "There is something strange going on here. I mean you look familiar but your eyes, I remember your eyes were a lighter brown… or am I imagining that?"

"Oh no! I used to wear colored contact lenses." Again she started to laugh. "I have to call my sister. This is so bizarre."

"Wait, wait." I shook my head trying to clear the cobwebs. "You are the corn dog girl?"

"What a small world… would you like our fresh cut fries with your corn dog? ha-ha-ha-ha…"

That was it! That is what she would always say when I bought a corn dog. This was proof positive. But how could this be happening? I find this girl, well this beautiful young lady that I had run into many years ago and she was helping me set up my 'happily ever after' home. How much more surreal can this get?

I looked at her. She at me. I knew at that moment this was meant to be. Call it fate; call it perfect timing; call it pure luck; I am calling it God's timing and God knew that right now, in this season of my life I needed someone special to complete my life. But how do I convey that to Prudencia? What if she doesn't feel the same way? She can't be in a relationship could she… I mean, she is in my car heading up to Colorado Springs… with me… uh-oh… time to end the internal-communication daydream before she finds me creepy.

"Well, this is incredible." I looked at her and we both shared a wonderful smile. "We better get up to the springs to grab some pizza. What a great surprise for me. I have thought about you quite often. Hope that's not a creepy thing to say."

"Okay Biff," I told myself, "just shut up and get going…"

"No Biff this is not creepy but it is so funny. My sisters and I always talk about that summer. You must have come by every day. We still laugh at that day we had to break the news that we ran out of corn dogs and were waiting for the delivery truck."

"I remember that!"

I put the car in drive and started to head to Fargo's.

"I was a bit disappointed."

"You think? You pouted as you walked away." Prudencia laughed and gently touched my hand. "My sister thought that was a sign you were gay. I told her you were sensitive."

"Sensitive, yes, I am sensitive."

Time to change the subject.

"So what keeps you here?" I asked.

"Well my family is here. I did a couple of years in the Army to finish my education and now, I have my own interior designing company. I normally work at redesign and updating hotels and restaurants in the region, but when you called I felt that you were a special case."

"Well I am incredibly thankful, especially since it is you."

"But now you know I will be expecting a twenty dollar tip."

She laughed and for once I felt an incredible peace.

We had a great evening at Fargo's and an even greater time continuing to reminisce on the trip back to Raton. Normally I would take the time to describe the wonderful dinner for two that comprised a medium "Lonesome Stranger" pizza that was made with lean beef, fresh onions and an incredibly generous amount of cheese on a perfect pizza crust. And normally I would brag about how the pizza was complemented perfectly by their fresh draft root-beer in the frosted mugs. And, I would go on to say, it all came to a perfect end with their "14-Karrot Cake" – But I don't want to take away from the romantic setting that was building.

We learned so much about each other and had such a great time that evening; I was convinced this was a Godsend. Moving to Raton was the right move. But for now, I would take each day one at a time and enjoy more of what God was planning for me. And, hopefully, she was feeling the same.

The work of redecorating and remodeling my new house began promptly the next morning. Prudencia arrived at the house around seven in the morning. I had a pot of coffee going and she informed me she had a crew coming for the construction part of the house. She had decided to limit my work on the remodel. She insisted on making it a more personal effort on her part so that she could surprise me at the conclusion of the project.

Over the next few days I was impressed at the kitchen appliances that were arriving and the incredible professionalism of the crew from Kitchen Solutions out of Pueblo, Colorado. The work was quick and far exceeded my expectations. Their foreman alerted me to a small problem that "in the long run may cause you some trouble." It was a plumbing problem and so I made a few phone calls and coordinated a plumbing repair job to coincide with the SCIF work Bernie was going to start in about three weeks.

In the end my kitchen was incredible. They pushed out a wall extending the kitchen to the West side of the house connecting it to an outdoor kitchen patio. This would allow me to grill while watching the sunset over the mountains that bordered Raton's west. Prudencia had ordered an apple red nostalgic refrigerator and matching Viking 48-inch gas range, dishwasher, and, of course a number of other Kitchen Aid products.

In my years of travels around the world I grew fond of cooking and it became a great hobby and source of relaxation. Some think this "fancy food" was more of an obsession. But, I just love good tasting food. So to see my dream kitchen become a reality was a great moment in my life. It was a milestone of sorts; my transition from warrior to civilian. But the greatest surprise was the hidden bar Prudencia had designed. It was next to the walk in pantry. Simply push the panel and a coffee bar rotated out that included an espresso machine, burr grinder, and a small one-pound home roaster for coffee beans. OH MY GOSH!!!

Prudencia also worked on all the other areas of the house and actually kept me out of the house for the last three days of the redecorating by getting me a room at the Holiday Inn Express (which made me wonder if she did like me since it wasn't a Marriott).

The result was magical. My house was truly a home and I felt so comfortable. I walked around looking at all the changes and additions. I was incredibly impressed with the quality workmanship and the attention to detail. My kitchen was, WOW! It was impossible to put into words.

The deck that came off of the kitchen area flowed seamlessly as if they were the same room. My living room looked like it was redone, but Prudencia pointed out it was only new window treatments and she had added a skylight. And my master bedroom was an oasis of its own with a relaxing bathroom area that included a soaking tub and steam shower. It was incredible.

After my first two nights in my newly designed home I could feel the change in my life. My body was finally starting to understand how to rest, and I found myself sleeping through most of the night. Of course getting used to the sounds of silence was going to take a few weeks, but once I am familiar with the local natural sounds, I would be able to relax and settle in at night without keeping my Glock under my pillow.

Over the next days I spent time in the kitchen testing out new recipes, much to the joy of Prudencia and ultimately her family who she took most of the cakes and pies too; I studied more about coffee and researched different roasting machines, grinders, brewers and, of course, I jumped online and ordered medium roasted coffee; and I even had some time to do some reading before Bernie's visit.

But more rewarding was the new friendship I had with Prudencia. We saw each other every evening. I would cook her incredible gourmet meals, and we would just sit out on the kitchen-deck sipping hot chocolate or a latte while getting to know each other. I even had her family over one weekend to "see her handiwork" a la my kitchen transformation. They were proud of her, it was clear to see. And they loved the meal I had prepared for them.

Life seemed easy but, I was still haunted by my past and was anxious about the visit from Bernie. And as promised he was there with a construction crew to upgrade my basement. The changes would mostly be internal with very little visible signs that the new room was in fact a government Sensitive Compartmented Information Facility. They installed a state of the art alarm systems and an electrical power scrubbing system not found in your typical home. This facility was all-weather, natural disaster proof, and had a back-up power system that would keep me functioning up to thirty days without support from the regular power grid. They also worked on what Bernie said was a necessary evil. It was a state of the art storage building that was also a garage. I figured there was more to it than that, but he wouldn't reveal anything until all the work was done.

One week later the work was completed and the briefings began. Bernie stayed a few days and we went over some information from human intelligence sources. What is so troubling about this information is how unaware the U.S. citizenry is to terrorism in our own country. Instead of addressing the growing problem of terrorism, our political leaders were trying to be careful so as not to offend Muslim's. The government just kept disregarding any warnings or indicators the intelligence community was alerting them to because they did not want to "alarm" the American public. I guess their motto was "keep them stupid; they will be easier to control." Sadly, much of America does not even realize how many terrorism attacks there have been in the U.S. partly because the media does not label them as terrorist attacks. But mostly because our politicians refuse to acknowledge them as acts of terror.

In 1972 ten members of a local mosque in New York City phoned in a false alarm and then ambushed responding police officers killing one and injuring three others. In 1973 there were nineteen deaths in the U.S. in the name of terrorism at the hands of Muslim extremism. 1974 saw six deaths; 1980 – three; 1989 – one; 1990 – two and on and on until a large attack in 1993 when Islamic terrorists detonated a massive truck bomb under the World Trade Center killing six people and injuring over 1,000 in an effort to collapse the tower. And then there was quiet until September 11, 2001.

Since that horrific attack that killed thousands and toppled the World Training Center and damaged the Pentagon, Americans have been killed by Muslim extremists on American soil every year. And the media and every presidential administration has turned a blind eye. And here I sit, a man who has seen the ugly side of terrorism, now secluded in paradise staring at these reports in my secure basement wondering why I should even care. I have all I have ever wanted. But it kept ringing in my brain; the world is a dangerous place and now America was becoming a breeding ground for terrorism. And we are just letting it happen.

Don't get me wrong, terrorism comes in all forms and nationalities. Even President McKinley's assassination at the hands of Michigan born Russian-Polish anarchist is considered a terrorist act. But the Muslim extremists have moved their Jihad onto U.S. soil and now they are even training in America and are sworn to destroy us from within. It is their "calling" from Allah.

Just the thought of sitting back while the country is handed over to terrorists made me ill. I had to do something and while sitting in my SCIF staring at pictures of my past I was reminded of something very profound: one man may not be able to take on an army, but a pissed off fire team can change the world.

And with that I called Bernie who had left just one week before and told him that I had a plan.

So now what to do about Prudencia. We were getting close and the "love" word had been tossed around a few times and I even held her hand. Yeah, I know. Things were looking serious and I was torn between staying put or going on just one more mission. Just one more time to at least put a dent in this infestation of terror.

There were two ways to proceed: one – just up and go and not tell anyone where I was going; or two – read Prudencia in to the program I was about to establish. Let her in on the secret war against terror. Swear her to secrecy and let her know her silence would keep me alive. Honestly, not telling her would tear me up on the inside. But first things first. I needed to make sure I had the support of the ultimate fire team.

So I made a few phone calls.

Terrorism, U.S.A.

WARNING ORDER

After taking a call from Sanders, who continuously thanked me from taking him out of the death spiral he said Fort Myer had become, I checked my email for more information he had been putting together. Some of the information was common sense, some was new to me, and a few of the documents attached to the email actually blew me away. It was important that if I were to help the Task Force I had to open up a few doors for Sanders and crew.

My first call was to my best friend and colleague Ron Sheposh, who, as you can guess, was on board with anything I was planning. He did remind me that I owed him a couple of favors and asked if this time I was going to pay up. I assured him I would and told him to stand by for a location and time to meet.

"So Biff, who you working for now?" Ron's voice echoed letting me know he was probably talking to me from the phone in his bathroom. Don't ask me why, but he had insisted on having a phone next to his toilet.

"Well Ron, this is a joint effort. But it will be my last one." I pulled the phone away from my ear as Ron busted out with a loud and obnoxious laugh.

"You old fart!" Ron chuckled, "You say that every time and then you follow it up with a 'no, really. It is my last mission. I promise.'"

"Thanks for the reminder, Ron. Stick by your phone, I'll call you by the end of the week with the information."

"Alright bud."

And, of course, I heard the sound of the toilet flush.

"I will be waiting."

The second call was to an old operative that was with me at Dragon Fire for a couple of months while in Kuwait. Vance Singleton was an incredible analyst and field operator. His expertise was his knowledge of improvised explosive devices (IED's) and specifically, their use by terrorist groups.

"Vance, this is Biff Baxter."

I waited for a response not knowing if I had to remind him of our professional connection.

"Biff!" His excitement was refreshing. "Hey, I heard you retired is that true?"

"It depends, who did you hear it from?"

"Let me say it this way, Biff, he really admires you and told me a couple of days ago that you were going to be working as a consultant for us."

"Well, if you are saying 'us' you must be on a pretty nice phone."

I was hoping what was going to happen next would be a connection to a secure phone.

"Almost. Dial the same number but instead of 5848 dial 8138."

You could almost see his smile from the sound of his voice.

"Roger that. Talk to you in a few." I hung up and redialed the new number.

"Counter Terrorism Center, this is Vance Singleton how can I help you?"

"Well, it works, how about you initiate from your side." I wanted him to initiate activation of the secure phone connection so that I could verify the signal was coming from a legitimate SCIF. And there it was, confirmation through the words scrolling across the display on my secure phone: *TS SCI – CTC USMA – DOD*

"Vance, great to talk with you. Got you TS."

He was acknowledging that are phones had just synced on a secure voice network and we were cleared to talk at a classified level up to Top Secret.

"Same here, Biff. So, you are with the CIA now?"

"Is that what my phone identifier reads?"

"No, but Bernie Griffin has been working with us on some analysis and he said you might be calling over here. I am up here at the U.S. Military Academy with the CTC. I love it man."

"Do they work on Dragon Fire stuff up there too?" I asked.

"Not too much. Dragon Fire had gone away for a while but looks like through fiscal CPR she's coming back to life. And the intelligence is still pouring in. Especially from some of your old assets. So are you retired or what?"

"I think I have one more mission in me, Vance."

"You will never change, Biff. There will always be one more mission for you."

"Well, this is it for me. I found a nice place to exist and I want to enjoy it."

"So, boss man, how can I be of service?"

"Vance, I have been reading some files about terrorism cells operating in and around Chicago. I believe one of the reports went as far as saying it was a training center for al-Qaeda, what is your take?"

"Biff, that is a hornets' nest. Not only is al-Qaeda operating out of Chicago but it is being supported by some heavy hitters in the political and financial arenas. And there doesn't seem to be a clear way to destroy the link. We have tried a lot of stuff."

"Who has tried to stop it?"

"The NSA for one. They have relentlessly tapped phones, intercepted radio communications, satellite transmissions. You name it they have heard it but when they try to issue arrest warrants it falls dead and they get in trouble for spying on citizens."

"Wait a minute. The NSA has intercepts of communications from Chicago to verified and known al-Qaeda sources and no one is acting on that intel?"

"You got it, Biff. The damn DOJ is blocking everything."

"The DOJ? Are you implicating the Attorney General?"

"No, no, no."

Vance's voice now became a calm and controlled whisper. "Biff, there are some strange things going on at the DOJ. It's not the attorney general, but staff within. Right now we have a few leads. But the damndest thing is we uncovered an al-Qaeda cell that has brought supporters together in a very prestigious university."

"Gee, let me guess... an Ivy league mill that turns out lawyers?"

"Yeah! How did you know?"

"Actually a lucky guess. There is no way terrorist would infiltrate an South East Conference school. Or even a Big Eight or Twelve school. My second guess would have been California."

"Well, your guess is good. We received a report from a fairly reliable source that we are still developing. He is a part of the group. He claims they want to control the DOJ."

"Vance, why would they want that? Is the DOJ that powerful that terrorist would want to take it over?"

"Biff, if the DOJ was run by an al-Qaeda sympathizer there would be little to no prosecutions on a federal level against them. They could reach their holy goal of inserting their way of life into America."

"They could get sharia law considerations in our courtrooms!" I shook my head in disgust.

"Bingo! The holy war these fanatics have declared for centuries has not changed. If you will not adhere to sharia law then you will be killed."

"Vance. We need to meet. When and where can we get together?"

"Bernie said to issue you a badge, so you tell me when and you can come out here and check out the center your old boss built."

"That's a great idea. I miss the old days working for General Downing."

"Yeah. Great man."

"You got that right, Vance. Let me call you in a couple of days. I have a few more calls to make. And I think I need a shot of Jack Daniels after what you just told me."

"You got it. Just call me if you have any other questions."

"Hey you never told me the university where this terror cell is located."

"Well, they are not terrorists, just a bunch of young college kids who are sympathizers. But anyway, it's Columbia."

"Columbia University? Are you sure?"

"Yes. But keep that under wraps. Just between you and me for now. The rest of the team here knows it but no one outside of CTC."

"Man, I do need that drink now."

"Great talking with you, Biff. Can't wait until you come out here."

"I am looking forward to it. I will call you soon Vance."

I hung up the phone and got up to take a break. I made sure all electronics were off and after locking the SCIF, I walked upstairs to grab a bite to eat and pour myself a good strong drink. It was mind boggling how corrupt our university system has become. They are cesspools of anti-American activities. I understood the protests during Viet Nam and even some of the protests against the efforts in Iraq. But to support terrorism groups like al-Qaeda was illogical. What would posses anyone to support a maniacal group whose entire works were aimed at killing indiscriminately just because you didn't want to conform to their way of believing? Even the Borg of Star Trek fame had more compassion than al-Qaeda.

This was frustrating, but at the same time, fed into what I wanted to propose to Sanders and Bernie. We had to get inside one of the terrorism cells operating out of Chicago and destroy it from within. Which, oddly enough, was the same tactic the radical Islamists use when toppling governments or disrupting societies.

I whipped up a BLT. But not just any BLT. First I placed four strips of thick bacon in a pan and sprinkled them lightly with brown sugar and a hint of cinnamon and then commenced to fry it. Next, I toasted two pieces of rye bread. While the bread was toasting and the bacon sizzling, I broke out the miracle whip and mixed it with horseradish and a pinch of smoked paprika and set it aside. I found a firm tomato and cut off two nice slices. I grabbed some whole leaf lettuce and plucked off one long leaf. Once the toast was done, I generously slathered the whip mix and set the two slices of bread on a paper plate where I assembled the sandwich. Tenderly, I placed the tomato slices equal distant from the edge of the bread and then laid the lettuce leaf over them. By that time the bacon was ready, and after I patted them down with a paper towel, I carefully placed them across the lettuce and set the other slice of toast on top to seal the deal.

I allowed the sandwich to sit a few seconds while I poured two fingers of single barrel Jack over three cubes of ice and then slowly poured two fingers of ginger ale into a tumbler.

I walked out to the patio and sat down to enjoy my lunch when my cell phone rang. It was Prudencia. I needed to hear her voice after the afternoon I was having.

"Hey Biff. I was checking to see if you were home."

"Yes, I was just sitting down to some lunch."

"Great! I wanted to borrow your culinary skills. Can you make a cheesecake for me? I wanted to take it to a friend's baby shower."

"Um, sure. When did you need it?"

"How about five?"

"Today?"

"Yeah, is that a problem?"

Okay sport, here is the bottom line on Prudencia; she is a great looking gal and a delight to be with especially since she was above average in intelligence and actually knows the difference between to – too – two and their – there – and they're. Unfortunately, just like most people in New Mexico, she didn't know much about cheesecakes.

"Well Prudencia, it takes an hour of prep time and three hours of cooking and then cooling it down. There's no way to make one today."

"Oh…" although I couldn't see her I knew that her puppy dog eyes were in full effect.

Just like Prince Charming coming to the rescue I offered up a life-line. "How about a Kahlua Coffee Cake? I have the stuff to make a Bundt cake, and I can have it ready for you by that time."

"Really? You are a life saver!"

"No problem. Just call me before you come over so I can have it wrapped up."

"Thanks, Biff. Love you."

"Love you too."

I hung up and realized the "L" word had been uttered and reciprocated. Was it genuine or did we just say it as an automatic response to the situation? And did she realize we used those words? I took a bite of the sandwich and for some reason the bacon tasted even better than ever. I savored every bite of my sandwich and every sip of my afternoon cocktail. With each bite I imagined Prudencia's face and her reaction when I give her the cake.

Maybe she'll kiss me… holy smokes! Was I back in high school or what? Why did this woman have this effect on me? Was this truly love? I took another bite of the sandwich to remind me what love was. Then a sip of the Jack and Ginger. Ahh, so wonderful!

I sat there for a while looking out in the distance as a golden eagle circled nearby. The sounds of silence were replaced by a symphony of happiness in my soul. Boy, things were so good right now. Why would I want to walk away from this?

I went into the kitchen and gathered the ingredients for the cake. Turned on the radio for some ambient sound as I started to work on the culinary treat I was making for my, er, for Prudencia. I mixed the ingredients, placed the cake in the oven and set the timer. I still needed to make my last call in my attempt to set up the team I needed for my plan to destroy the terrorism effort in the U.S. but I decided to wait until the cake was out of the oven. I didn't want any distractions that might cause the cake to burn.

As the cake was baking I stepped out on the porch and did a little target practice with my Remington 700 (it is actually an M-24A3 SWS with a Leupold Mk 4 LR/T M3 10×40mm scope that fires a .338 Lapua Magnum. But for legal reasons, let's just call it a Remington 700). I had set up a few targets at 100, 200, and 300 meters and since I lived "out in the country" I was never bothered when I shot my guns.

I was tempted to shoot the rabbit that was out by the 200 meter target but decided to just keep lead on the targets. I loved to shoot my weapons and inhale the smell of the gun powder. Just a comforting feeling. After about 45 minutes later, I heard the oven alarm go off, so I cleared my rifle and set it on the dining room table as I tended to the cake. It looked perfect. I set it on a cooling rack and took my rifle downstairs to store it. I would clean it later. It was time to make more phone calls.

My last call was to my intelligence source David Shelton. This call was going to be the toughest since he made it clear he was upset last time I called him. But I played it smart and got on his good side by not using my cell phone. Instead I was calling him from the encrypted phone. This should give him a sense of security and would win me some trust points.

"Biff, I am not sure I can help you much. I can't risk sending you any more intelligence reports." Dave sounded unsure and very cautious.

"No worries, Dave. I have all the reports I need. Do you think you can fly out for a vacation weekend? My treat."

"Where are you, Biff?"

"Dave, don't try to trace me. I am in an agency SCIF. Can you come out and look a few things over with me?"

"I will come talk but I can't promise anything yet."

"No problem. I would like to fly you out to Denver this weekend. Are you available?" I sat there pulling up flight information for flights out of Charleston, South Carolina into Denver.

"Denver? Your phone says Clarendon, Virginia. Biff, who are you working for?" Dave sounded really distant and put off by the fact he couldn't get a trace on my phone. It also made me wary.

"I told you it's an agency SCIF."

I paused to take a deep breath and a quick check of my senses. This was not panning out like I had hoped and something was just not right. Time to cut this short.

"Look Dave, forget about it. I am sorry to have bothered you." I hung up and immediately pressed my ghost button. This was a button on the phone that allowed me to stay connected to Dave's phone and eavesdrop on any conversation he had after the hang-up. It worked two ways: if he simply hung up I would be able to hear anything he would say for up to one minute, and then I would be disconnected. But if he called someone I would be able to hear his entire conversation. It was a parasitic phone system that allowed the monitoring to stay alive as long as there was an active connection. Once the connection was broken, there was the one minute ghost period. But the great thing is the entire process was recorded.

I listened as he hung up the phone. I heard him mutter over and over 'this is not happening. This is not happening' and then some shuffling of paper after which he picked up the receiver and unfortunately for our friendship, he placed a call – and I listened:

Ring, ring.

"Come on pick up." This was the voice of a man in great distress. *"Pick up…"*

"This better be good." The voice of a woman. Not immediately identifiable.

"We have a problem."

"I have no problems, Dave. You on the other hand are crossing the line calling me at this number, and looking at the display, calling me from a government phone. What kind of an idiot…" she was interrupted by Dave's haunting words.

"Biff just called me."

"What did you say?" the anger in her voice was unmistakable.

"Biff just called me and tried to invite me out to Denver to talk. He said he was working for the agency."

"What agency? Who is he working for? What is he working on?"

"All he said was he was in an agency SCIF. And then he hung up after I asked him who he was working with."

"Is there anything else Dave. I am a bit concerned that someone with your background could not figure out where he was calling from."

"The phone display said Clarendon, Virginia."

"Clarendon... Clarendon." This woman was deep in thought.

"Dammit Dave, here is what needs to happen. You need to find him and you need to find him now! If he finds me we will all go down. I did not build this to have some idiot allow it to be destroyed all because he failed basic phone conversation skills. If he finds me, you are the first to go." Her chilling voice was not just threatening but extremely haunting.

"Don't threaten me Tina. If he finds you it's as much your fault as it is mine. I am cutting all communications with him."

"No! If he calls you again you WILL agree to meet him. He must go and the only way to accomplish that is for you to meet him and take one of my Tiger teams with you; they won't let me down. Don't call me again unless it is to tell me Biff is dead."

The phones went silent and I sat there as the reality of what I just heard set in. The female voice was that of rogue CIA operative, Tina Ferguson, who had been on the run since the Dallas showdown. She had eluded the FBI's search for her and now her web of evil was entangling an analyst working with the Department of Defense. She may have just placed me on a hit list but the advantage is mine. I now knew her next move, and I knew how it would go down. The insane part is that it seemed to be another door that could lead me to the growing terrorism problem in the United States. But why was she still in the U.S.? After Cuvellier International went down the FBI figured they all went overseas. They fled like roaches running when the lights are turned on in the kitchen (not my kitchen but most restaurants).

I saved the audio tape and then transferred a copy of the audio file to my laptop and then another copy to an external hard drive. I sat there for what seemed an eternity just staring at the computer screen. I opened up the internet browser and checked a few news sites. Not really reading or comprehending what I was looking at, but just staring into the screen almost like the time I stared as the medevac that took off with Ysabel de Haro after she had been injured in our mission in Central America. I came out of my trance when my cell phone started ringing. It was Prudencia telling me she was on her way over to pick up the cake. I shut down the computers and locked up the SCIF and turned on the alarm. I called the alarm company out of Colorado Springs to let them know I had just armed the SCIF Alarm and then I headed up the stairs.

I went straight to the kitchen and started wrapping up the cake for Prudencia to take to her party. I was a bit worn out having just experienced this act of betrayal and defiance. I was also trying to figure out how to handle this situation. Do I call Bernie, and get him involved, or do I just handle this on my own and invite Dave out to Denver and then let him know I am on to him? In the old days I would have just worked him over, but I needed to get on the inside. I needed to find out just how extensive this network of evil actually was. Whatever I decided, I needed to do it soon. But in the meantime, I would plan my trip to New York for a sit-down meeting with the CTC folks, I may be able to think more clearly once I get an overview on what I may be facing.

After a few minutes of staring out the window, Prudencia pulled into the driveway and I found myself smiling as my eyes followed her every step as she walked toward the front door of my house. She saw me as I was staring through the window and waved while dazzling me with a great smile. She was wearing black, somewhat faded jeans, a red pullover sweater with a black, gray, and white design of what looked to be Scottish terriers, black ankle boots and her hair pulled back with an almost invisible headband. I met her at the door where we embraced.

"You act like you haven't seen me in years." She teased as we broke the embrace and started to walk to the kitchen.

"It has been a long day." I laughed and pointed to the cake that I had placed on a Swarovski crystal cake platter and covered with colored plastic wrap.

"Wow! Not only are you a great chef but you are fancy too." She was clearly impressed as she took possession of the platter and held it up inspecting the goods.

"You shouldn't have covered it though?" she looked a bit sad as she looked at me with her declaration.

"Why? I thought you would like the fanciness?"

"I'd rather be able to taste the cake." She laughed as she started to unwrap the cake.

"STOP?" I took the cake from her.

"I made you a sample cake," I said.

"Shut up! Did you really?" She clapped her hands signifying she was happier than a fat kid in an all you can eat ice cream store that was giving away unlimited free samples.

I went to the counter by the oven where I had made a mini-Bundt cake just for the sampling.

"Here you go," I smiled as I grabbed a fork and walked toward her carrying the cake.

Prudencia was already sitting on one of the bar stools at the kitchen counter when she jumped unexpectedly; startling me to the point where I almost dropped the cake and grabbed the pistol I had hidden in the breadbox on my kitchen counter.

"Oh, I forgot." She exclaimed "I have my new assistant in the car."

"Prudencia, you just set me back ten years. Holy smokes, girl!"

"Let me go get her. Do you mind?" She asked looking over her shoulder as she was walking to the front door.

"No not at all." I turned and walked to the bar and poured myself a drink… no, not Jack and Ginger, heck, I am not a lush, just a glass of cranberry juice.

…With a little vodka.

…And a twist of lemon.

…Shaken.

…Poured over ice.

Prudencia walked in with a younger lady with incredibly blonde hair. I have never seen hair that was so blonde it was almost blinding.

"Biff, this is RuthAnn Ronaldo; RuthAnn this is Biff."

"Hi Biff, nice to finally meet you. You are all I hear about."

Slightly embarrassed I grabbed her hand and tried to say something nice in return.

"Well, it's all true if it was good. So how long have you been in the design world Ms. Ronaldo?"

I asked as I went to the cupboard to grab a plate and another fork.

"I am just starting. Economy is a bit tough and Prudencia offered me some part-time work helping her out. We've known each other a few years."

She sat at the counter, and I started to cut the sample cake to serve the two ladies.

"Prudencia, what would you like to drink?" I asked.

"We will just drink water. We can't stay too long. We have to be at the baby shower in one hour."

"So RuthAnn, where did you meet Prudencia?"

Always good to get information about someone while they are distracted, in this case by incredible food.

"I worked at the pharmacy. Goodness! Did you really make this?" RuthAnn was inhaling the cake and leaving no crumb unattended.

"Thank you. So, did Prudencia come in a lot for samples at the pharmacy?"

I chuckled but due to her reaction or lack thereof, it was either an old pharmaceutical joke or just not funny.

"Biff, this is very good. Thank you for making it for me. I really appreciate it." Prudencia turned to RuthAnn, "He is a wonderful chef. Maybe you should come over for dinner one weekend."

"Sure RuthAnn, come over some time and we will do some grilling. Thanks to Prudencia's great design I have the best indoor and outdoor kitchen in the world." I pointed behind them where the kitchen was separated from the outdoor grilling area by sliding glass doors.

"I would like that. Thanks."

Prudencia finished her cake and got up to take her plate to the sink. She grabbed RuthAnn's plate too.

"Hey, Biff, how about next weekend? Let's have some people over next weekend." Prudencia smiled as she stopped by my side and gave me a hug.

"Not too sure about that yet. I need to fly to New York very soon and was hoping to get it out of the way next week."

What a great time to let her know I was going to be gone for a few days.

"Oh, when were you going to tell me about that?" Prudencia loosened the hug and looked up at me with sad eyes.

"I was just invited today. I was going to tell you this evening."

"So Biff, what do you do for a living?" RuthAnn finished her water and was now standing as the two ladies were getting ready to leave.

"I am retired from the military so every now and then I do some consulting. I am going to the United States Military Academy at West Point to visit an educational center out there."

"That is impressive. I have an old friend who graduated from West Point. He's still in the Army, I think."

"Well, it is a tough place to get into but those guys that graduate are top notch. Can't get a better education." I started to escort the ladies to the door when a novel idea hit me.

"Hey Prudencia, why don't you go to New York with me? I can take you on a tour of the city and then we can hang out in Times Square."

I was smiling at my great idea.

"That might be a good idea."

Prudencia's smile let me know that I made a great move asking her to join me in New York in front of her friend.

We got to the front door and was opening the door when Prudencia asked:

"Um Biff, aren't you forgetting something?"

Oh, my goodness. Here it was. The moment I had been waiting on… my first kiss with Prudencia. But dang, I thought it was going to be all private and special. Maybe after a nice dinner or walk in the moonlight. But, oh well, a kiss is a kiss so I stepped forward to prepare for the kiss.

"Yeah, we can't forget the cake." RuthAnn chimed in.

"Oh, let me go get that."

I ran to the kitchen, grabbed the cake platter and took it to them as they had already made their way down the front stairs and were moving toward the carport.

"Here you go."

I handed Prudencia the platter, and she carefully placed it on the back seat of her car. RuthAnn had gotten in and was buckled up. Prudencia closed the back door and was getting into the driver's seat.

"Thanks Biff, I will see you tomorrow."

And she kissed me on the cheek.

"Enjoy."

I just waved as she drove her car around the carport and made her way down the driveway.

SECRETS REVEALED:

GAME ON

As I had explained to Prudencia, I had to take a short business trip to New York. Unfortunately, her schedule could not allow her to go with me. She insisted on house sitting and offered to take me to the airport. When I told her I would just leave my car at the airport she insisted I drive her car and leave it at the airport and of course she would take care of "Felicia" my corvette. Yes, she gave my car the name Felicia because she said it was the name of a girl who was both beautiful and strong. I just laughed and agreed.

I know what you are thinking, why would I let her babysit my corvette? Well, they say love is blind, and maybe, this time, it was really love and I didn't really care about my material possessions, just my happiness and making her happy. Or maybe I am just stupid. So I drove her, wait for it, light red Volkswagen Bug – yes, America's top super spy was driving a pink VW Beetle from Raton to the Sun Port International Airport in Albuquerque.

I was able to get a seat on a United flight from Albuquerque to LaGuardia by way of Chicago. At least I could grab a Chicago Dog during my layover at O'Hare. Had my layover been in Dallas I could have grabbed some doughnuts at Dunkin' Donuts, but as luck would have it, those flights were booked. The flight to Chicago was without incident, and as planned I took in the culinary fare made with the one and only Nathan's Hot Dog Links. After eating the tube from heaven and fighting myself from consuming a second one, I made my way to the gate and, no surprise to me, the information board warned us lowly travelers that we would be experiencing a delay.

The delay set me back an hour and a half. The flight finally touched down at LaGuardia around nine at night making my drive in the rental car to Fishkill, NY an adventure to say the least. I hate driving to Fishkill at night because once you are out of the city, those roads get extremely dark… and then there are the toll booths, but I will save that rant for later.

It was Sunday night and my first meeting with the CTC was Tuesday. I, as tradition had it, stayed at the Residence Inn by Marriott in Fishkill where I settled in for a good night's rest.

The next morning I started out my regular New York routine with a short run and very light upper body stretch in the Marriott's workout room. Not that I was a big fitness nut, no, I just knew I had better get the metabolism going if I wanted to participate in my New York specific eating tasks like my long-awaited visit to a local bagel shop. Interesting fact for you East Coast citizens wishing to visit New Mexico; there are eleven bagel shops in the entire state and only a handful of Dunkin Donuts so bagels are scarce.

After a fairly nice sweat session, I showered and headed off to grab some circles of pleasure…this time it was one of my favorite stops: The Bagel Shoppe in the Fishkill Village Square near Main Street and Blodgett Road. I ordered their plain bagel with cream cheese and a lemon poppy muffin with a cup of coffee. I took my food outside to enjoy the beautiful morning.

If you ever get out to Fishkill you will be surprised at its quaintness, if I can use that word. It blows me away that such an unassuming town exists so close to the chaos of the Big Apple. But there she sits, seventy-miles north of Queens and just twenty-miles away from West Point. The beauty of the mountains, the trees, and even the beauty of the Hudson River just make this town a little slice of heaven.

After my filling breakfast I went back to the room to study up for the meeting with the CTC. I had to remember that most of the work done there was from the viewpoint of the academia versus the operational intelligence that I was used to collecting. Simply put, this means that instead of reading raw intelligence reports I would get to read reports subjected to the analysis of guys behind desks that probably never spent a day in the field environment. The task at hand would be to discern intelligence from speculation and useful information from fabricated considerations based on an analysts 'hunch'.

Nonetheless, I also wanted to spend time getting to know the crew at the CTC, so that I would be able to provide them with any actionable intelligence should I run into any during my quest. I guess you can say I was the collection manager asking the analysts for their intelligence requirements.

After a few hours of 'what-if-ing:' "what if this", "what if that," "what if I drove myself crazy"... enough of that. I decided to take a trip out to West Point to make sure my arrival in the morning would be without incident or delay. The drive was uneventful but stunningly beautiful. I made mental notes of the two Dunkin' Donuts along the route and a few historical and tourist sites I wanted to visit.

I arrived at the town of Highland Falls and followed West Point Highway to the Military Academy entrance. No problem with the security guards since I did produce the correct identification however I was advised of another entrance that would cut my drive by about fifteen minutes. I opted to stay my course and allow myself the opportunity to visit the shops in Highland Falls as well as the West Point Museum.

As I drove around the campus and took in the incredible views of the Hudson River there was turmoil brewing inside. Tomorrow morning I would be researching the latest information of terrorism in the United States. For many years the Department of Defense had talked about preparing for a terrorist attack. But the intelligence community had another view on terrorism. Especially when I was with TF Dragon Fire. We weren't worried about an attack; we were worried about the reality of the invasion of terrorist organizations throughout the America's and the next morning, my worst fears were confirmed.

I had a fairly restful night, and I started my morning with a stop at a Dunkin' Donuts on my way in to West Point. I ordered up a large coffee with cream and sugar and a blueberry cake doughnut and a Bavarian cream filled donut. Oh, my goodness! I was in sugar heaven, and the coffee was always a pleasure to drink. I made it to West Point despite the urge to turn around and go hang out at the doughnut shop. Heck, you would have thought I was a cop or something.

I parked near the Baseball Field on West Point and walked to the Counter Terrorism Center where I was met at the front door by Vance Singleton; an old friend and a great American.

"Biff! Man the years have kicked your ass."

"Thanks Vance. I think. You look good man, how have you been?"

"Busy, Biff."

He grabbed my arm and pulled me away from the building.

"Sure thing Biff, I will show you around," I looked at him puzzled.

We crossed the street and walked along the sidewalk towards the Library. I remained silent and pretended to look around as if on a tour.

There were very few cadets walking about as classes were in session. We finally stopped in front of the statue of General George S. Patton positioned by the library. History tells us Patton never even visited a library during his years at West Point.

Vance looked up and pointed to the top of the library. "Two guys came to the CTC this morning unannounced. They claim to be from the CIA, and when I asked them if they worked with Bernie Griffin, they had never heard of him. But they said they were the counter terrorism analysts for Middle East and Africa."

"Are they still there?"

"Yeah. Their credentials looked legit, but I was not going to chance it. The information I have for you has been seen by very few. And once you see it, you will understand the ramifications if anyone with malicious intent were to get hold of it."

"Some damning evidence?" I looked at him as a cadet was walking towards us.

"Information that would bring down high powered people if not our government."

The cadet passed by not knowing if he was supposed to salute or not so I feigned a salute and, as automatically as you can get, he snapped a salute hollering 'bandits, sir.'

"You're such a jerk, Biff. Well, once these clowns showed up I went for a little walk and put some stuff upstairs for you to read. You have a few minutes?"

"Of course. Are we going into the library?" I looked towards the magnificent building where our future leaders spent countless hours studying.

"Yes sir. Hope you ain't allergic to a library like General Patton claimed to be." He mustered a smile and a laugh.

I laughed too, but in the back of my mind I was busy trying to imagine who the fake 'CIA' guys were or if in fact they were fake. It is not like the agency to send 'analysts' to a place like the CTC without an invitation. It was pretty scary to think that if these guys were imposters that their credentials were so tight it fooled a strict security force.

The library was incredible. Six stories and almost one-hundred-fifty thousand square feet of learning. The library housed over a half-million books and about twenty-thousand government documents. Couple that with historical artifacts, an advanced Center for Teaching Excellence and a one of a kind Center for Enhanced Performance and you have the greatest library in the college ranks. And possibly the top ten among all libraries in America.

We went up to the fifth level where Vance had reserved a study room. In the room were a few binders marked For Official Use Only. I sat at the table and he stood near the door as I looked over the documents.

I was right. The documents were the work of analysts who were opining on the raw intelligence they had received either via classified channels or open sources. The reports were incredibly well written and sadly, almost shockingly eye-opening. Some of the information was old news to me but a few documents took me by surprise.

Terrorist organizations had been moving into South America and Canada with boldness and purpose. Great numbers of Muslims established cities in the Western Hemisphere. The South American city of Ciudad del Este held a large Arab population and had escalated in growth in the late 1940's. The Iranian-backed Hezbollah militia established this base camp in the South America, country of Paraguay. The city had been the financial center for a growing force of Islamist radicals who were "boiling with hatred for the United States and ready to die to prove it," according to one of the militia members sited in one of the documents.

The State Department had put out travel warnings to diplomats and U.S. businesses to steer clear of the Tri-Border area comprising Ciudad del Este, Foz de Iguazu, and Puerto Iguazu. Three cities that border Argentina, Brazil, and Paraguay. But this was not where all the action was. This area was a staging area. Their priority was to attack the United States should any harm come to Iran. These terrorists had been entering the U.S. for decades and setting up training areas; courting and establishing financial backers; firmly defining supply routes; and recruiting college students.

A report citing some CIA documents singled out the Mexican border as an especially inviting thoroughfare for Hezbollah operatives. According to one source, "Many alien smuggling networks that facilitate the movement of non-Mexicans have established links to Muslim communities in Mexico."

"Non-Mexicans often are more difficult to intercept because they typically pay high-end smugglers a large sum of money to efficiently assist them across the border, rather than haphazardly traverse it on their own."

Most of the Hezbollah operatives that make it in to the U.S. make their way to Chicago, Detroit, Boston, New York City, Seattle, San Francisco, Los Angeles and Washington D.C. Those with a financial background, anyone with experience as a CPA or bookkeeper, are moved to Chicago. Those who are gifted or trained in explosives go to the West Coast while those with mechanical or specialized training go to the East Coast.

Already, these operatives had been responsible for hundreds of murders throughout the western hemisphere and have become a strong force financially by working with drug cartels throughout Central America and distributing cocaine and marijuana in the U.S., Canada, and Europe.

I closed the binders and realized my worst fears. They ARE here. The terrorists had invaded the U.S. and it was just a matter of time before they made their move to take over the government. I got up and walked to where Vance was standing outside of the room.

"Only one question for you, Vance."

"Follow me to the upper level first. I need some fresh air." Vance gathered up the binders and documents into a bag and then led the way up to the observation deck.

We stood along the wall looking out to where the Hudson river took a turn south. Many people do not understand the importance of the hallowed grounds of West Point. West Point's role in our nation's history dates back to the Revolutionary War, when both sides realized the strategic importance of the west bank of the Hudson River. General George Washington considered West Point to be the most important strategic position in America. Washington personally selected Thaddeus Kosciuszko to design the fortifications that make up West Point in 1778, and then Washington transferred his headquarters to West Point in 1779. Continental soldiers extended a 150-ton iron chain across the Hudson to control river traffic. West Point is the oldest continuously occupied military post in America.

I took in the history, and then my thought turned to one of the notorious names associated with the history of West Point – Benedict Arnold.

"Vance, what do we know about high level political figures associated with the terrorist cells out of Chicago?"

"One of my guys is placing that document in your suitcase in your room as we speak."

Vance laughed and looked at me with a great big smile.

"I do believe I just Biff Baxtered you."

"That's pretty good, Vance."

I gave him a man hug.

"Hey where can we get some coffee?"

"You're right, coffee is needed and right now, Biff. We'll just walk down Thayer Road and head to the Cadet Restaurant. They have pretty good food there, too, if you want."

I took one last look at the beauty of the Hudson River and walked back into the library where we took the elevator down to the first floor and walked, as he said, along Thayer to the café. We went in and I decided I would get a bite to eat so I grabbed some fruit, a cup of yogurt, and of course a cup of coffee.

We sat down in one of the booths against the window and silently ate our food. My mind just whirring about what our country was experiencing with no one noticing. I sipped my coffee, which wasn't too bad as Army coffee goes, and looked at the young faces that were trickling in to grab a bite to eat between classes. Some sat down and studied. Some walked around in khaki pants and polo shirts and acted goofy. I figured them to be the seniors or Firsties as they are called at the Academy, since they were the ones that were acting like second lieutenants.

"I wonder if they really know the world they are about to inherit." I asked Vance as I ate my last cantaloupe cube.

"Well, Biff, if you are about to do what I think you are about to do… it won't be too bad."

Vance smiled and raised his coffee cup for a toast.

"What are we toasting Vance?"

"To the Corps of Cadets and the nation they will soon be defending."

"To the Corps."

Almost as if on cue my cell phone rang. I looked at the caller ID "Prudencia"…

"Hey Prudencia, what's up?"

"Biff, are you okay?" her voice clearly shaking with fear.

"Yeah, are you okay? You sound upset."

"Oh, Biff, someone broke into your house and tore things up and they stole your car." She started to weep and her words were not audible.

"Slow down and take a deep breath. The most important thing is, are you okay Prudencia?"

"I was hiding in the spare bedroom…"

"Prudencia listen. Listen!"

My voice raising as if that would make her listen faster.

All cadet eyes turned to watch the drama unfolding in their eatery. Vance, seeing the situation was getting tense, urged me to stand and head outside. As I walked towards the exit Vance scribbled a note to me that read, *'whatever you need I will get for you.'*

"Prudencia, you need to call 9-1-1 and tell them the brownstone is broken. Do you understand?"

"What does that mean, Biff?"

"Darn it, Prudencia, listen to me. Just tell them the brownstone is broken and I need you to go to the shed behind the house. There is a key in the kitchen drawer where the butter knives are kept."

"A key in the drawer," Prudencia was repeating my words as she was evidently rummaging through the drawers in the kitchen. "Okay, I have a silver key."

"Good, hold on to the key and call 9-1-1. If they ask you for a code read the numbers printed on the key."

"So you want me to call and tell them the brownstone is broken and I have the code here."

"Yes! And get out of the house now! Call me after you call 9-1-1."

I hung up and started to pace along Thayer Road while Vance was getting on his phone barking orders.

"Okay Biff, I have a guy heading to your hotel room packing your stuff up and retrieving the package I had them place earlier."

"Thanks Vance. I have to get back to Raton immediately."

"I have a plane standing by." Vance was on his A-Game and I saw that warrior fire in his eyes. "Let me make one more call and we will be on our way."

Prudencia was calling.

"Are you okay sweetheart?" I asked trying to keep calm.

"For now, but you have a lot of questions to answer."

"Sure, sure, sure."

I had to stop the rambling so I could get her out of there safely.

"Okay Prudencia, head to the shed. The combination to the door is the number on the key."

"I guess this is a key, key."

Her attempt at humor was comforting but clearly a defense mechanism masking the fear she was clearly experiencing.

"Prudencia, I am one of the good guys. Those people that broke into the house are not, and I need you to leave and head to my hide spot."

"What hide spot?"

"Are you at the shed yet?"

"Yes, and now I am inside the shed. What is this?" Prudencia had discovered my survival shed and, most likely was impressed.

"This is my get away equipment. Stand in the square in the middle of the floor."

"The square with the skinny table?"

"Yes, that one." There was no other square but clearly she was doing her best to stay calm.

"Okay Prudencia, now place the key in the key hole on that skinny table and turn it clockwise."

"Okay, I'm turning the key."

"Hold on, it is an elevator."

The elevator lowered Prudencia into an underground garage. Almost like the bat cave only this one was for real.

"Biff, are you a spy?"

I laughed as the words came over the phone. No one had ever asked me that before and it really sounded funny.

"Sort of, I guess. Let's just say I have lived a very interesting life. Now take the key and step off the lift and walk towards the car."

"I'm at the car and the lift is going back up."

She was clearly looking around taking in the hidden retreat the SCIF team had built just in case of emergencies like this. Only it was intended to be used by me, not my girlfriend.

"The car you see has the key in it. Get inside and follow my instructions exactly, do you understand?"

"Biff, do you love me?"

What is wrong with women? Why is it in the middle of great and fantastic moments in life, or heck, even in history, do they have to mess with a man's mind? Did Nancy Reagan ask Ronald if he loved her while he was demanding the Berlin Wall be torn down?

"Prudencia, I love you more than you can ever imagine. And because I love you I want you to live. To live you have to do everything exactly like I am going to describe. It will not make sense to you and will go against all logic but you must do everything exactly like I tell you. Can you handle that?"

"Tell me again." I could hear her getting into the car.

"Okay, you have to do every..."

"No! Tell me you love me." Her voice still held a hint of uncertainty and fear.

"I love you Prudencia Sarkisian and when I get there I will hold you and never let you go."

"Okay. I am ready."

Really ladies? Is this how the female mind works? I shake my head in utter confusion.

"Okay, babe. By my instructions and with no questions. Are you ready?"

"Yes. What kind of car is this?"

"That's a question Prudencia. We are not supposed to have questions remember?"

"I just wanted to know."

"It's an Isuzu Amigo. No, it is not a gorgeous car but it is about to save your life. Now, love-of-my-life, if you are ready…"

"Sorry. I am ready."

"Start the car."

She hesitated, and I knew she was thinking how dangerous it was to start a car in an enclosed area.

"Trust me."

I heard the Amigo start up.

"Like I said, babe, you have to trust me. Now press the green button on the dash." As she did the onboard computer came alive.

"Unrecognized driver. Password please."

"Say Infiltrate, Observe, Report, Evade."

"Infiltrate, Observe, Report, Evade." I could imagine her gripping the wheel repeating the words, probably not even realizing what the words were and hoping nothing bad would happen.

"Welcome friend. Please state your name."

"Just say your name."

"I am Princess Prudencia." She said loudly and then whispered in the phone, "I might as well have fun."

I laughed as I heard the computer greet her, *"welcome princess. Your destination please?"*

"Say safe house Bison."

"Really Biff? Oops. Safe house Bison."

89

"Safe House Bison has been programmed. Please proceed to the door marked 'C'."

"Okay, Prudencia, now comes the crazy part."

"And all this hasn't already been crazy?"

"Oh, you have no idea. Now just drive towards the door marked 'C' and let the conveyor system catch the tires. It will pull you out of the garage."

"Now you are scaring me."

"No worries really, sweetheart. There will be a heads-up display. Just get on the conveyer and put the Amigo in neutral. You can even stare at the map while it moves you out of the garage. The car will do the rest."

"Okay I am on the conveyer thingy and the car is moving towards the wall."

"That's good. Don't do anything. As a matter of fact, maybe you should close your eyes."

"Why?"

The angst was increasing and she was not handling the car situation too well.

"What if I keep my eyes open?"

"You will pee your pants."

"I trust you, Biff. None of this makes sense, but I trust you."

She started humming an unfamiliar tune

"Biff? The car is turning."

"Yes, the wheel will turn itself for a few more minutes."

"Oh, my gosh, this is so scary yet so cool."

"Well get ready because once it gets you out of the garage it will be your turn to drive."

"I am outside of the building now and it is still steering. Is that okay?"

"Yes. It will do that for another minute or so. I am very proud of you."

I was smiling picturing her innocent face. The lovely smile. I just felt so bad that she was put in this spot.

"Um Biff. There is no road here."

"Are you okay with roller coasters?"

It was a bit late to ask but she would have panicked had I asked her earlier.

"I'm closing my eyes again! Oh, oh, oh!"

And there it was, the ear-piercing scream of someone on a rollercoaster. The computer was navigating the Amigo down an almost 35 degree paved surface that resembled turns 8 and 8a at the Laguna Seca Race Track just outside of Monterey, California. Most racing aficionado's know this section of track as the corkscrew. Hence, the scream by the princess.

"Are you okay?"

I almost laughed but realized she had never had to escape like I have had to do.

"OH, MY GOSH, BIFF!"

She was panting and clearly the Amigo had come to a stop.

"We stopped. We stopped."

"Okay. In the center counsel is some bottled water. Take a sip and off you go. Just follow the GPS map and call me if anything happens."

"Biff, tell me now, are you a spy or something?"

"Or something... Prudencia, I love you. I will see you soon. My friend is flying me out. The computer will guide you to the hide house. Once you get there call me."

"I love you, too."

I hung up and looked at Vance.

"Dude."

Vance was laughing and crying.

"She is going to kick your butt. You didn't tell her what you do? That is so dang funny."

"I was about to tell her after I talked to you but she had to run off and do something and... dang, she's gonna kill me."

"Well, come on let's go. We have to meet the guys at Stewart Airfield."

"What guys?"

"Well Jim, one of my coworkers, went to get your stuff at the hotel. And then there is Keith Heffner, our pilot. He'll take us to Raton."

"You said us. Are you coming with me?"

I was hoping he would. There was too much to talk about, and I was sure Prudencia wouldn't hit me in front of people.

"If it's okay with you?"

"How does the CTC get to have a pilot and a plane?"

"Oh, that's not CTC. This is agency stuff. I have been working here as their liaison. I just couldn't tell you before. Don't stress out, Biff or I'll have to break out the tranquilizer darts."

Vance laughed as we walked towards the Grant Turnaround, a place where cadets frequently had pizza or Chinese food delivered during long study nights. One of the cadets' favorite restaurants, Dong Fong (a.k.a. King's Garden), was just a hop, skip, and a jump from the Highland Falls gate but because of limited driving privileges, cadets would wait at the turnaround for delivery of their favorite Asian delights.

A car was waiting to take us to Stewart Airfield. Shortly before boarding the agency plane, I sent Bernie a text about the car and the break in. He responded that he was sending a team to see what they could do to recover the car "gifted" me by the agency. This thing was fully computerized but, of course, all the real sensitive stuff was removed, but the covert GPS tracking systems was still engaged so finding it would be as easy as finding a cop at a doughnut shop.

Terrorism, U.S.A.

THE FLIGHT OUT

Upon initial observation, the safe house looked like a regular house in Northeast New Mexico. No special architectural structures or exotic landscaping, just a regular home tucked away in a draw exactly eight miles west of Raton Municipal Crews Field. The airport serviced the Raton area, the NRA Whittington Center, and, of course, late night flights bringing in special operations soldiers who surreptitiously trained East of Raton.

The house had been used over the years by the special ops teams and also served as an isolated interrogation center for different intelligence agencies. Once the Amigo's computer was activated to provide the route to the safe house an National Security Agency computer alerted the Intelligence Watch Team operating in the Pentagon that the safe house was about to be occupied. This triggered a series of events that included: turning on special security cameras, audio recording devices, and placing a security team on standby that just happened to be based out of the Whittington Center.

Once Prudencia arrived at the house the computer would direct her to provide the access password. That is when I anticipated a phone call from her asking me what to do. As usual, I was right. I passed her the password and gave her special instructions to only enter the bedroom marked with a number 3 and the kitchen. I told her that every word and movement was being recorded and should she enter any other room she might get shot.

Normally, an author would love to tell you the great things she saw and the procedures she used to get into the house, but had I done so, this book would not have been cleared by the "censors" if you know what I mean. Suffice it to say, she did get in, grabbed some food from the kitchen and took it to the bedroom that had all the amenities of a five star Marriott. Television, phone (guarded), couch, bed, kitchenette, drinks, and even a full bathroom with a Jacuzzi tub and a change of clothing for both male and female occupants.

I called the team responsible for security at the Safe House and was relieved to know they were members of a Polish security team normally responsible for security of Rail and Port facilities in Poland. One of the senior members was a young lady I had heard about but never met, Aga Jagodka. Aga was a senior operator on a special security operations team for the Rail transportation system. It was Poland's version of Special Weapons and Tactics (S.W.A.T.) for their countries internal security. She was kind enough to head over to the Safe House and see if Prudencia needed anything.

Vance had asked Keith Heffner, or "The Heff" (as I was advised to call this Wildman they had as a pilot,) for an estimated time of arrival. We were flying with a pretty nice tail wind and making great time so he said he would have us wheels down at approximately 9 PM mountain standard time. Not bad considering this was an unplanned flight and everything was thrown together in the blink of an eye. The Heff had made it known the great sacrifice he had made to make this trip happen. Something about "a once in a lifetime dinner with three New York Giants cheerleaders in a loft apartment in Manhattan." Maybe I could make it up to him with a steak and Green Chile burrito and a bottle of Mountain Dew.

Vance and I read more documents, and I asked tons of questions. Tired from the reading, I kicked off my shoes and stretched out for a quick nap. It is amazing the recollection the mind experiences as you settle in for rest. There were numerous times I had found myself in private jets battered and bruised as I completed one mission just in time to begin a new adventure. There were many hours of angst and uncertainty traveling at 35,000 feet and being nursed to health by beautiful women. (All of those ladies turned out to be rats.)

My minds trip down memory lane started to take a nasty turn as I remembered the deception and dishonesty of my former friend Uwe Cuvellier. How the dark side of terrorism turned a great man into a no-good piece of garbage. And, then, there was my latest foe, Tina Ferguson who probably was building a web of killers to further her reign of terror. She had already eluded the CIA and FBI. She even had an FBI Agent, Margie Gross, working with her. I met Margie during my last mission and thought it was the start of a great friendship. But the evil forces of terrorism and the allure of great amounts of money helped turn Margie to the dark side. There was no way of knowing how far Tina's influence had reached. But this was proof that the terrorism world was well financed and that they were not afraid to spend money to continue their infiltration of America.

I sat up as a chill ran up my spine. I looked over to Vance who had nodded off. I got up and walked to the back of the jet where I found the galley and poured a cup of coffee.

"I'll get that for you, sir." The charming voice of a young lady startled me causing me to jump back and assume a modified horse stance.

"Where the heck did you come from?"

I half hollered causing Vance to wake up and jump out of his seat.

"I didn't mean to startle you," the young lady somewhat giggled as she cautiously poured a cup of coffee. "I am Sara, Mr. Singleton's assistant."

"Sorry about that, Biff," said Vance as he came around the corner.

Vance came to the back of the plane just as I was coming down off of personal Def-Con 5. Sara handed me the cup of coffee, and I immediately took a sip.

"Dang Vance, what the heck man!"

I was shaking and had to sit down.

"I totally forgot, Biff."

Vance held a coffee cup as Sara filled it for him.

"Sara has been with the agency as long as I have, and I just forgot to tell you. I am so sorry."

"No problem Vance. I think I just might have a Xanax in my bags somewhere."

"Mr. Baxter would you like a light snack? We are still a couple of hours out."

Sara opened a cooler and pulled out some cheese and vegetables and started to assemble a snack tray.

"Sure, Sara, that would be great."

I took another sip of coffee truly enjoying the great taste.

"What kind of coffee is this?"

"It's a little something I picked up during my last visit to Mexico. It is Maragogype, a seasonal coffee that is pretty hard to get in the states." Sara was pleased that her choice of coffee was a hit but something about her told me she wasn't there just to serve coffee.

"So what do you do for a living?" I asked.

I watched as she finished placing some ranch dressing in a small bowl and set it in the middle of the snack tray. Vance sat across from me shaking his head and smiling.

"I am an operative." Sara said in a terse and clear voice.

"Biff, you never turn it off do you?" Vance was now laughing.

"How did you even think to ask her what she did with the agency? She told you she was my assistant. Most people would have left it at that."

"Well, after she startled me, I was ready to immobilize her. But I noticed that either she has prosthetic hip or she is carrying a Ruger, possibly a 380, and her hand was just inches away from grabbing it."

"Are you kidding me?" Sara was stunned.

Slowly she reached for her pistol which was a new Ruger 380 Auto that she had just picked up during a trip to Arizona.

"How can you know that just by...?"

"Don't try to figure him out, Sara." Vance interrupted. "He's Biff Baxter."

I stared at her while sipping my coffee.

"It's a gift. Oh, and Vance isn't wearing underwear."

We all laughed, but inside I was still trying to calm down. I grabbed a celery stick and dipped it into the ranch dressing. Munching on it I asked

"So what is your assessment on the terrorism problem in the U.S.?"

Sara looked at me and then Vance. She picked up a square of cheese with a colored toothpick and slowly bit it in half.

"Mr. Baxter, we are just months away from becoming a third world nation. The terrorists are here in America and, under the guise of political correctness, they are winning. They are having their way with America and our inept leadership is allowing them to take over this country." Sara sat down next to me with a cup of coffee.

"And if I can be open with you, and please, nothing against you, there is nothing we can do to stop their hostile takeover."

"Why do you say that there is nothing that can be done to stop their takeover?" I interrupted.

I finished the coffee just in time for Vance to get up and pour me another cup.

"The radical Muslims have already had cases in court overturned because the U.S. laws conflicted with their Sharia Laws. The beastly man who beat his daughter in public because she brought shame to their family for talking with a boy was acquitted because 'their religious beliefs' allowed for this form of correction. Unfortunately the young lady will never walk again but it's okay because Muslim law says it is so and it trumps our laws."

"How bad do you think it will get?"

I looked into my cup of coffee as if a magic answer would appear and I would be able to fix the situation.

Sara sighed.

"Our laws were based on our Christian beliefs. Every law based loosely on the Ten Commandments. By the year 2020 we will no longer be a Christian nation and the Ten

Commandments will be null and void. Our laws will be end notes to new laws that will have all Americans adhering to the laws of these Muslim infiltrators."

Sara stood and looked me in the eyes.

"In short Mr. Baxter, the America we grew up loving and enjoying is dead. Christianity is gone and we will be ruled by Muslim law. The disgusting part is that these terrorists will lie, cheat and steal their way into the White House and America's citizenry will be too stupid to see it coming."

"Biff, I am sorry," Vance started to apologize as Sara walked toward the front of the jet.

"Sara has been adamant about al-Qaeda getting someone into the White House. We have no solid intel that this is going to happen or that the White House is even their goal."

"No solid intel?" Sara asked in disbelief.

Sara had returned with a folder and a book.

"The proof is right here."

She tossed the book onto the table in front of me. It was a Quran, the Muslim book of faith. She then handed me the file folder.

"Go ahead and open it up but the bottom line is we have career politicians that have sold their soul to the Muslim faith and they will lie to destroy their enemy. The Quran says there are two forms of lying to non-believers that are permitted under certain circumstances, *taqiyya* and *kitman*. These circumstances are typically those that advance the cause Islam and in some cases by gaining the trust of non-believers in order to draw out their vulnerability and defeat them."

"So, I see that you have researched this thoroughly."

In the file folder she had brought back was a list of students and faculty at several universities that had been contacted by different al-Qaeda associated organizations.

"Sara has a theory that America is being set up like the people of Mecca were set up in the days of Muhammad."

Vance poured himself another cup of coffee and filled my cup again too.

"You will have to fill me in. I am not familiar with that story." I said.

Sara now knelt beside me almost as if she were ready to beg me to help her.

"The Muslims will lie to get what they want[viii], and though not called *Taqiyya* by name, Muhammad clearly used deception when he signed a ten-year treaty with the citizens of Mecca that allowed him access to their city while he secretly prepared his own forces for a takeover. The unsuspecting residents were conquered in easy fashion after he broke the treaty two years later, and some of the people in the city who had trusted him at his word were executed. I submit to you that we will live those days here in America."

I sifted through some of the other papers in the files we were looking at earlier. I picked up one of the papers and looked it over again. It was a paper written by analysts who had interviewed prisoners being held in Guantanamo. It read:

Yassir Arafat was famous for telling Western newspapers about his desire for peace with Israel, then turning right around and whipping Palestinians into a hateful and violent frenzy against Jews.

The 9/11 hijackers practiced deception by going into bars and drinking alcohol, thus throwing off potential suspicion that they were fundamentalists plotting jihad. This effort worked so well, in fact, that even weeks after 9/11, John Walsh, the host of a popular

American television show, said that their bar trips were evidence of 'hypocrisy.'

The transmission from Flight 93 records the hijackers telling their doomed passengers that there is "a bomb on board" but that everyone will "be safe" as long as "their demands are met." Obviously none of these things were true, but these men, who were so intensely devoted to Islam that they were willing to "slay and be slain for the cause of Allah" (as the Qur'an puts it) saw nothing wrong with employing Taqiyya in order to facilitate their mission of mass murder.

The Islamic Society of North America (ISNA) insists that it "has not now or ever been involved with the Muslim Brotherhood, or supported any covert, illegal, or terrorist activity or organization." In fact, it was created by the Muslim Brotherhood and has bankrolled Hamas. At least nine founders or board members of ISNA have been accused by prosecutors of supporting terrorism.

Prior to engineering several deadly terror plots, such as the Fort Hood massacre and the attempt to blow up a Detroit-bound airliner, American cleric Anwar al-Awlaki was regularly sought out by NPR, PBS and even government leaders to expound on the peaceful nature of Islam.

"Sadly this is making sense."

I placed the paper down and rubbed my eyes both out of fatigue and frustration.

"So, Sara, Vance, how do we stop this?"

I looked at the two of them for answers but was not ready for what I would hear.

"Biff, we can't stop it without a major war. And it will be a Holy War that may just end in an apocalyptic fashion. The main effort of al-Qaeda in the west has been under the guise of being the peaceful people of the Muslim brotherhood. They have entered the United States almost undetected." Sara's solemn look was shared by Vance.

"I was in on some of this back in 1997." I said.

I thumbed through the files but couldn't find anything relating to what I was about to share.

"What do we know about the Hezbollah presence in South America?"

"It is only growing."

Sara finally took a seat almost as if in defeat. She stared down at the ground.

"Sara, this is very troubling to you isn't it?"

I stared at the pained face of this intelligent woman.

"Biff, no one has taken this threat seriously. Mostly because money is what moves our politicians and money is what the terrorist have tons of available to them at the drop of a hat. The NSA even tracked money trails to many of our high ranking politicians. Even to the office of the past Presidents."

"Are you telling me Clinton and Bush are funding the terror effort?"

It was an incredible revelation.

"I am telling you that agencies associated with them have, either unwittingly or purposely, funneled money to Hezbollah, Hamas, al-Qaeda, you name it, they have received money from our leaders."

Sara looked up and stared in my direction as if I were transparent.

"What is your concern with South America?" she asked.

"Well, back a few years ago when I was on assignment down there, a person of interest passed me a list of confirmed Hezbollah operatives trying to gain access to the U.S. Of the seven on the list, only three were stopped and never given a visa. The others entered the country and disappeared."

"Hate to break this to you, but that is an all too familiar story."

Sara stood and started to gather up the files that we had spread across the table.

"I will venture to guess there is anywhere from ten to fifty thousand people in the U.S. with direct ties to one of the terror organizations. Add to that those indirectly associated with terror and we have the population of a city the size of San Antonio or Portland."

The three of us sat there in silence. Only the sound of the jet engines moving us effortlessly through space and time. My mind was racing – is this too big to engage? Should I even try? And then it hit me; you can't stop something that isn't moving. The answer was not to stop the growth of this terror, but to keep it from growing. Like the old saying of "fighting fire with fire," maybe the answer was to fight terror with terror. A plan started to form in my mind. The plan would need the help of my old friend, Ron Sheposh.

We landed at the airstrip that was adjacent to the Raton airport, and I called Prudencia to let her know we would be there momentarily. We walked toward an SUV that was sent to meet us when we noticed another vehicle pulled up joining the party. Clearly it was unexpected since the team with the SUV reacted defensively.

The SUV turned a floodlight on to the new vehicle while two of their men, security detailers, drew their weapons and demanded the vehicle occupants to exit the vehicle with their hands up. A tense situation compounded by the thick accent of the Polish security detail.

Vance, Sara, the Heff and I stood back while the drama unfolded. With no shelter or barricades between us and the two vehicles, we were frozen in our tracks, vulnerable to whatever was about to happen. Almost like an East German caught in "No Man's Land" near the Berlin Wall.

The unknown vehicle turned off their lights and the front passenger door opened slightly and two hands made themselves visible as they were extended upward through the opening.

"It's Bernie. Bernie Griffin. C I A."

"To jest w porządku, że jest z CIA" it was Aga who had been part of the security team.

I walked toward her to introduce myself, but as I approached she introduced herself to me.

"Biff Baxter, great to meet with you. I am Aga Jagodka."

"Aga," I hugged her. "It is a pleasure to finally meet you. Cieszę się, że cię poznać... is that right?"

She smiled.

"Mr. Baxter, you are very impressive but we will work on pronouncing the words."

The team gathered their bags and loaded them onto the SUV. Bernie joined us and we discussed the procedures to enter the safe house compound.

"Good to see you Bernie. I want you to be with me as I talk with Prudencia. I am not too happy about this, but I do believe I have been compromised."

I was a bit disappointed but we had to figure out who would have broken into my home.

"Don't sweat it Biff. We have a team tracking the 'vette and some more information Sanders brought with him."

He pointed back to his vehicle.

"Well, let's get to the safe house."

SECRETS REVEALED:

SAFE HOUSE BISON

We boarded the vehicles and the security team took charge of the plane and secured it into a special hanger after fuelling and a quick maintenance check.

We got to the safe house and followed Aga's instructions as to who stayed in which room. I was looking for Prudencia, and when I finally saw her she just openly wept and I held her for a long time, not saying a word.

Prudencia finally looked up at me and smiled "I'm dating a spy."

"No, that was the old me. I just consult. Listen, it's very important that whatever you see you cannot talk about."

I kissed her forehead.

"Why don't you get some sleep? We may be here a couple of days until we figure out who broke into my house."

"Okay. My new friend gave me some sleeping clothes." She pointed to Aga who just smiled back and walked over to escort Prudencia to her room.

Bernie gathered his files and with Sanders, Vance, and Sara walked into a room with a table. I joined and we started to unfold some of the events from the day.

"Well, we know Biff's house was broken into and it is no coincidence that it happened while he was in New York getting briefed up." Bernie looked at the group. "Biff, the agency has a team in your house and they have been lifting prints for the past three hours. They will run prints as they get them and I will be alerted to any hits off of our databases."

"What's the latest on the corvette?" I looked at Sanders.

"The good news is the corvette has been located. But the bad news is, despite the fact that we told the Deming police that the FBI was on their way, they have already started going through the car because, and I quote, 'there is something fishy about this car'."

"Deming, New Mexico?"

I was running a map in my head.

"Yes, sir. And they are morons. FBI arrived there about an hour ago and almost arrested the police chief for obstruction. Turns out, they may have disassembled part of the car."

"Vance, Sara, Deming is a border town. Do you think there is a chance they were trying to cross the border?"

"Sounds possible especially given the technology in the car."

Sara opened a file she had brought with her.

"There is a big need for advanced GPS technology for both drug cartels and terrorists. What do we know about the driver or any other vehicles traveling with the corvette?"

"That's the part that really frustrates us." Sanders continued. "There was a van that actually pulled over with the corvette but the police officer waved him on. The same van came and hung out at the police station for hours."

"And the driver?" Vance asked.

"In custody with Deming police. I will send a text to the FBI agent and ask for the latest." Sanders got up and pulled his cell phone out of his briefcase and started texting.

"Since we are all up what about a quick update on what we are trying to accomplish?"

Bernie looked around to get approval to give us a briefing.

"It's almost 10 PM, let's hear a little while we wait for an update from the FBI on the corvette." Vance spoke in agreement with the rest of the team.

Bernie started his review:

"In July 2007, seven key leaders of an Islamic charity known as the Holy Land Foundation for Relief and Development (HLF) went on trial for charges that they had provided material and financial support and resources to Hamas, a known foreign terrorist organization. They were accused of money laundering and breaching the International Emergency Economic Powers Act, which prohibits transactions that threaten American national security. The surprising thing is that along with the seven named defendants, the U.S. government also released a list of around three-hundred co-conspirators, who were never indicted, and a group of business professionals joined in, what they called 'joint ventures.' During the trial, many incriminating documents were entered into evidence. But the most significant of these was this one."

Bernie held up a document that was well bound and looked like it could be a fairly long read.

"The document is 'An Explanatory Memorandum on the General Strategic Goal for the Group in North America,[ix]' authored by Muslim Brotherhood operative and Democratic National Convention fund raiser Mohamed Akram. The FBI found Akram's memo in the home of Ismael Elbarasse, a founder of the Dar Al-Hijrah mosque in Falls Church, Virginia. Elbarasse was a member of the Palestine Committee, which the Muslim Brotherhood had created to support Hamas in the United States. Akram's document, published in 1991, listed the Brotherhood's twenty-nine 'organizations of friends' that shared the common goal of dismantling American institutions and turning the U.S. into a Muslim nation. These 'friends' were identified by Akram and the Brotherhood as groups that could help convince Muslims that their work in America is a kind of grand Jihad in eliminating and destroying the Western civilization from within. Their task was "infiltrating and sabotaging America's, quote, miserable existence," end of quote, by their own hands so that God's religion, Islam, is made victorious over all other religions."

"We have found that this organization, the HLF, was the nucleus of terrorist activity in the United States. However, the threat is not as much them as the Muslim Brotherhood who is calling all the shots and, oh by the way, there are a plethora of U.S. lawyers, accountants, and politicians tied to the Muslim Brotherhood."

"Hold on, Bernie." I stood and started to pace. "You are telling us that this brotherhood has been active for years; you have intelligence that tells you this; you have names; and they are still around? That's not what I expected. Why haven't all these people associated with the brotherhood been deported or placed in prison?"

"Biff, the Muslim brotherhood has been courting the United States since the 1950's. Presidents, members of congress, all of them were duped into believing this group was formed to promote good will to all in the name of Allah. They have been very convincing in their rhetoric and very charismatic and charming to everyone they meet. They were very believable, and that was their plan. Akram was well aware that in the U.S., it would be extremely difficult to promote Islam by means of terror attacks. So they came up with the 'grand jihad' where he and his brotherhood comrades overtook the infidels without the violence of bombings and shootings, but rather a stealth or covert jihad aiming to impose Islamic law, what we call Sharia Law. This was their plan to unify and direct Muslim efforts in business, society, and politics; and to present Islam as a civilized alternative to a democratic society. At its heart, Akram's document details a plan to conquer the United States and turn it into an Islamic state. And they weren't going to stop there, the U.S. is not their ultimate objective. Conquering the U.S. is only a stepping stone toward the larger goal of one day creating a worldwide or global Islamic state."

I looked around the table to see glazed over eyes. And not from the lack of sleep, but from the shock of hearing that America has been under covert attack since the 1950's. What the heck are our politicians thinking? And why hasn't anything been done to stop this attack?

"Bernie, that still does not answer my question. Why does this continue?"

"Biff, the Islamic Brotherhood is running much of our country. They have some heavy hitters under their control.

And sadly, money talks." Bernie shuffled some papers and then walked to a refrigerator where he grabbed a bottle of water while bringing a few more bottles and setting them on the table where we were assembled.

"Bernie, to quote my good friend Ron Sheposh: 'give me a list of names and we will take them out.'" I opened a bottle of water and took a drink as the anger built in my soul. I was so furious and wanted nothing more than to wipe out these clowns and then go hide in a secluded area and become a hermit.

Sara chimed in: "why don't we call it a night and tomorrow morning we can further explore the problem and come up with solutions."

"You know Sara," Vance jumped in, "I would agree except this is only the tip of the problem. Let me add this so that we can mull it over in our sleep. The brotherhood decided to establish Islam and the Islamic movement within the United States, so that the Muslim religion could be 'enabled within the souls, minds and the lives of the people of the country.' [x]They are convinced that this could be accomplished through the establishment of firmly-rooted organizations that build the confidence of the masses through community care and welfare programs. In other words, they become such a strong and successful presence in the U.S. that people will associate Islam with success and care. They have been urging Muslim leaders to make a shift from the attack and kill mentality to the absorption mentality, meaning that they should abandon any tactics involving defiance or confrontation, and seek instead to implant into the larger society a host of seemingly benign Islamic groups with superficially unobjectionable motives; once those groups gain a measure of public acceptance, they will be in a position to more effectively promote a fundamental transformation by using the old Communist technique of 'boring from within.'"

"The heart and the core of this strategy, is contingent upon these groups' ability to develop a mastery of the art of building or establishing coalitions. That is, by working synergistically they could complement, augment, and amplify one another's efforts."

Sara had opened a file and raised her hand.

"It was Akram that is credited in saying: 'The big challenge that is ahead of us is how to turn these seeds or 'scattered' elements into comprehensive, stable, 'settled' organizations that are connected with our movement and which fly in our orbit and take orders from our guidance.' So to him the ultimate objective was not only a huge Muslim presence, but also the implementation of the objectives of the Muslim Brotherhood of transforming America's pluralistic societies into Islamic states, and sweeping away Western notions of legal equality, freedom of conscience, freedom of religion, and freedom of speech."

She slammed the file shut and you could see the disgust in her face.

"Look, I can understand this strategy but the U.S. is so diverse, they will never be successful." I looked around at the group. "Look at us; we all have different likes, tastes, hobbies; how can they even think they can 'change America' with our great diversity. And let me remind you, the South will rise again according to our Alabama brethren."

The group laughed, but it was not enough to take away the anxiety that was building because of this intelligence dump.

Bernie stood and stretched. "Let me sum it up with this: Akram and the Brotherhood understood that in order to succeed in this endeavor, they needed to appeal to different layers of the American population in different ways; that whereas some people could be influenced by messages delivered from a religious perspective, others would be more responsive to messages delivered by educators, or bankers, or political figures, or journalists, etcetera. That is why Akram's blueprint for the advancement of the Islamic movement stressed the need to form a coalition that covered a myriad of groups composed of every conceivable part of society. We have confirmed members of the U.S. Muslim Brotherhood coming from the worlds of education; religion; political activism; the entertainment world; print media; banking and finance; the physical sciences; the social sciences; professional and business networking; cultural affairs; the publishing and distribution of books; children and teenagers; women's rights; vocational concerns; and jurisprudence."

"So if this was Star Trek and we were up against the Borg, it is right to say 'we have been assimilated'." I asked.

I stood and stretched as the others followed suit.

We were all tired and ready for some sleep.

"One last thing, Bernie. And yes, I am ready for sleep. You mentioned groups in America that are assisting in this jihad. Do we have access to that list?"

I asked only to find out just who the evil doers were almost convinced that amongst them we would not see a bacon company.

"Let's attack this problem tomorrow. I have your good friend Ron Sheposh coming out. He will bring the latest intel and, some experts that will help us plan our mission." Bernie looked around at the group that was assembled.

Sanders' phone rang and everyone watched as he took the call.

"Yes, sir, I was the one who called about the status of the Corvette. Yes it is a government asset... I understand... great... Well if this is a good number for you I will text you the information..."

Sanders looked at me and gave me a thumbs up.

"Okay lieutenant, great work... oh yes, that's S-A-N-D-E-R-S Colonel United States Army... that is correct, the FBI has the rest of the information... okay, thank you."

"Well?" I was anxious to hear about my car.

"It is not damaged. It can be driven and they are contracting with the Army to deliver it to Raton in a couple of days."

Sanders smiled from ear to ear.

"Thanks colonel!" I shot him a quick salute.

"Well, as I was saying" Bernie brought us back to reality "Remember this: tomorrow the actions we take may very well be considered treasonous. We are going to expose the enemy that is within, and I dare say, those that have tried to bring it to the attention of the media and the lawmakers have all disappeared. Think it over because tomorrow there will be no turning back."

SECRETS REVEALED:

AUTHORS NOTE:

IN OUR WORLD WE MUST ACCEPT THE REALITY THAT THERE ARE
THREE SIDES TO EVERY STORY: YOURS, MINE, AND THE TRUTH.
RIGHT NOW THE POLITICIANS HAVE TRIED TO MOLD EACH PART OF
THE STORY TO FURTHER THEIR OWN AGENDA. HERE ARE THE
TRUTH'S AS WE KNOW THEM: (BY THE WAY, IF YOU TEND TO GET
UPSET AT THE TRUTH YOU MAY WANT TO TURN THE PAGES
QUICKLY OR FIND A STEPHEN KING NOVEL TO READ BECAUSE WHAT
I AM ABOUT TO DISCLOSE IS GUT-WRENCHING). AS YOU READ ON,
UNDERSTAND I AM BOUND BY NON-DISCLOSURE AGREEMENTS TO
NEVER DIVULGE CLASSIFIED INFORMATION. THE MEDIA OVER THE
PAST DECADE HAS SEEMED TO CAPTURE INFORMATION THAT IS
VERY CLOSE TO THE GROUND TRUTH AS KNOWN BY THE
INTELLIGENCE COMMUNITY. MOSTLY IT IS THE TRUTH THAT HAS
BEEN CLEARED FOR PUBLIC DISSEMINATION. THE REST OF THIS
BOOK TAKES A LOOK AT THE EVENTS AND ACTIVITIES THAT
OCCURRED LATE 2009 AND EARLY 2012. BUCKLE IN, THIS GETS
ROCKY.

AN AWAKENING

Circa 2011

The next morning I took time to get Prudencia settled into the reality that I was not your average boyfriend. I gave her the cliff notes version of what I did for the military and my brief encounters with evil while working with the CIA. She was impressed but at the same time concerned. She wanted to know how much longer I was going to do "this kind of work." I thought for about fifteen seconds, looked at the concern in her eyes and made her a promise I never thought I would make:

"This will be my last assignment; I promise you because I love you and never want you to worry about my welfare. I want to spend the rest of my life with you."

Tears glistened in her eyes.

I held her for a few moments and felt the tension leave every muscle in her body. We stared at each other, and I told her that once I got the word that my house was clear and secured, I wanted her to go there and relax. There would be a security detail in the shadows, but it was the safest place for her. And if she wanted, her family could join her as long as she never mentioned anything that had transpired.

I joined the others in the kitchen area where we chatted over some doughnuts and hot coffee. The chit-chat continued through the morning until Prudencia left with an escort to the house. I told her not to worry and that I would call her regularly. She smiled and kissed me gingerly on the lips.

"Biff, please be careful. I want to spend the rest of my life with you, too."

She held me close, and we jumped when a loud booming voice startled us.

"Good, Lord!" I yelled

"Biff you romantic old bastard."

It was Ron Sheposh. He had snuck up on us while I was helping Prudencia into the car.

"Ron, you're an idiot."

I walked over and hugged him and brought him over to meet Prudencia.

"Well missy, I cannot believe someone actually broke through this old shell and captured his heart."

He gave her a hug.

"Now, don't worry your sweet little head about Biff, he is with me, and I will make sure he gets to you safe and sound."

"Thanks Ron."

Prudencia got into the car and buckled in as the driver started it up.

"Dude, she is hot!"

Ron was gleaming.

"Ah, Ron, come on she can hear you."

I just shook my head.

Prudencia rolled up her window and blew me a kiss, "Thanks again, Ron."

I watched the car pull out of the compound not understanding why I would want to put her through this stress. She is truly a strong woman and I felt bad knowing I had placed her in such an awkward position. But unfortunately, I had a mission I had to complete. I glanced back as the car drove off and Ron and I made our way back to the safe house and met up with the others.

"Biff, look what I just pulled up."

Bernie had his laptop hooked into the flat screen in the living room and a document was up on the screen.

It was an analysis paper I had written just five years earlier when I was working with the Defense Humint Services (the original DHS – and as they say, NOTHING is as good as the original).

"I hope you don't mind, but I wanted to share this with the team. It has great insight and, quite frankly, I believe it is the reason they [the terrorists] hate you." Bernie left the document up on the screen as everyone started to read it.

AN ANALYSIS OF TERRORISM – COMPILED BY SFC B. BAXTER

The Middle East is a cesspool of evil and confusion. The confusion is partially the byproduct brought on by the unwanted assistance forced upon them by the United States and other Western Nations. For years analysts have been saying we have absolutely no reason to be injecting our two-cents into any of the disturbances over in the Arab World. We cannot try to affect change in a society where they have yet to fully accept their own identity.

What do I mean? Arab culture is a mixed bag of beliefs but to put it simply, a mixture of Christian and Islamic communities. The problem is the Islamic community has a radical sect that has taken on an identity of evil.

The true Islamic faith is based on the five pillars of Islam that define the duties by which every Muslim must live. After I discuss these five pillars, I will reveal to you the often debated sixth pillar that was added to the Islamic belief to satisfy a thirst for evil. These pillars, very similar to the Christian faith, are:

Declaration of Faith (Shahadah)

Prayer (Salah)

Charity (Zakah)

Fasting (Sawm)

Pilgrimage (Hajj)

Declaration of Faith (Shahadah)

The first and basic requirement to be a Muslim is to publicly state the words, "There is no God but Allah and Muhammad is His Messenger" in Arabic, with sincerity and without any reservations. This testament is the foundation for all other beliefs and practices in Islam. To become a Muslim, a non-Muslim must repeat the Shahadah three times in the presence of witnesses. This declaration of faith is as follows:

- **Belief in One God (Allah)** – Allah is one and has no partners or equals.

122

- ***Belief in the Prophets*** – *Allah sent prophets to every nation to provide mankind with guidance, so that they could walk the straight path of Allah, live happily in this world, and be prepared for life after death. The fundamental message of the prophets was identical: remind mankind of Allah's (God's) oneness, the reward of a good life, the Day of Judgment, and the fate of disbelievers.*
- ***Belief in the Holy Books*** – *Allah sent messages to humanity through His prophets. These messages are contained in the Holy Books of Allah:*
  - *The Suhuf (Scrolls), revealed to the Prophet Ibrahim (Abraham), and now lost*
  - *The Taurut (Torah), revealed to the Prophet Musa (Moses)*
  - *The Zabur (Psalms), revealed to the Prophet Daud (David)*
  - *The Injil (Gospels), revealed to the Prophet Isa (Jesus)*
  - *The Qur'an, revealed to the Prophet Muhammad (PBUH)*
- ***Belief in Angels*** – *In addition to the physical world we know, Allah created a world invisible to us in which angels exist. The angels are sinless. They require no food, drink or*

sleep. They have neither physical desires nor material needs. The chief responsibility of the angels is to praise Allah and to do his will. The most important of the angels is Jibr'il (Gabriel). On behalf of Allah, Jibr'il (Gabriel) revealed to the Prophet Muhammad (PBUH) his mission and the perfect verses of the Holy Qur'an. Each human being is assigned angels who serve as guardians and recorders of the individual's deeds, both good and bad.

- **Belief in the Day of Judgment** *– The belief of life after death and in the resurrection of the dead on the Day of Judgment is an essential part of Islamic faith. It gives meaning to life and sets the joys and troubles of this life into a much wider context. Any person who believes in life after death will be afraid of acting against the will of Allah. He will be conscious of the fact that Allah is watching all his actions and the angels are recording them.*

- **Belief in Fate** *– Everything that happens is the will of Allah and is preordained. Acceptance of fate is an essential element in submitting to the will of Allah.*

Prayer (Salah)

Every Muslim is required to pray five times a day. These five prayers are said at dawn, mid day, late afternoon, sunset and nightfall. The Prophet Muhammad (Sal Allahu Alayhi Wa Sallam) said, "The first act that the slave (of Allah) will be accountable for on the day of judgment will be the prayer. If it is good, then the rest of his acts will be good. And if it is evil, then the rest of his acts will be evil."

Charity (Zakah)

Every Muslim is obligated to pay a portion of his or her wealth for the benefit of the poor and needy. Zakat means purification and growth. Our possessions are purified by setting aside a portion for those in need. This also increases social welfare and encourages economic growth. A Muslim may also donate more as an act of Sadaqah (voluntary charity), in order to achieve additional reward from Allah.

Fasting (Sawm)

Every year in the month of Ramadan Muslims are required to abstain from food, drink and sexual intercourse from dawn to dusk. In addition, Muslims are expected to refrain from anger, envy, greed, lust, gossip, violence, bad language and other inappropriate thoughts and actions. Fasting is meant to encourage Muslims to seek nearness to Allah, be patient, and learn the hardships faced by the less fortunate.

Pilgrimage (Hajj)

Hajj is a pilgrimage to the Holy City of Makkah (Mecca). Hajj occurs every year during the month of Dhu'l-Hijjah. Every Muslim who is physically and financially able is obligated to perform Hajj at least once in his or her lifetime.

Where, in any of this is built in hatred? NOWHERE! This is the innocence of Islam that many scholars will defend. But while they are defending this part of the faith, they neglect to point out the radicalization of the faith with the addition of a twisted sixth pillar of belief. That sixth pillar is JIHAD.

Optional 6) The Shia faith believe the sixth pillar is khums, which means that believers have to pay about twenty percent of your wealth to the Sayyids. However, some Sunni minorities such as the Taliban and Al-Qaeda, view that jihad is the sixth pillar of Islam, and newer groups that want to renew the definition of the pillars of faith, such as Islamic Jihad and Hamas, favor this belief of jihad as the sixth pillar.

A few Muslims, mainly some Kharijite groups in ancient times and members of Egyptian Islamic Jihad have taught that Jihad should be considered the sixth pillar of Islam. In this context, Jihad is viewed as external war against those perceived to be enemies of Islam.

Now to be clear in the historical context of these groups, the Kharijite group was strongest

around the 7ᵗʰ century when this group of
angry people started to question the rulers of
the Islamic nation and started a revolution in a
struggle for political power after the death of
the Prophet Muhammad. Today, remnants of
this group exist in Algeria, Tunisia, Libya and a
great majority in Oman.

The Egyptian Islamic Jihad, on the other
hand, you may have heard of because in 1998
they were formally merged into al-Qaeda.
Anyone reading this surprised? The group that
has reigned terror, chaos, death and
destruction around the world has continued the
work of the Kharijite Group. It was the writings
of the early Kharijites that popularized, or
made common, the desire for martyrdom and
dying for the sake of God.

To sum it up, Sunni Muslims (the majority of
the Islamic nation) believe there are precisely
five Pillars of Islam, and as such Sunni leaders
teach there are only five major pillars of the
faith. Traditionalists say that no sixth pillar
should be added, because changing the pillars
would be altering the religion and its beliefs,
and so anyone who believes that there is a
sixth pillar is committing a sin. Thus, Sunnis
believe that a 'six pillar of faith' is outside the
folds of mainstream Islam. The sixth pillar of
Islam is not included in the Sunni way of life.

The radical Sunni's are the ones who reach
back to the writings of the early Kharijites that

calls for sacrifice of one's life for Allah. So where does that leave us? The minority of the Islamic nation have made the sixth pillar of Jihad something which the world now is dealing with on a daily basis. This warped belief system is not only dangerous, but it is not being addressed by the United States government as wrong. We skirt around the truth and allow this rogue belief to grow. But then again isn't that how we operate in America? The majority is almost always silenced and the minority, with backing by special interests, rises to make the rules for the rest. [xi]

"Biff, do you still stand by this?" Vance looked at me almost like a coach about to put in a kicker for the winning field goal.

"I do, but with some additions. First and foremost, our battle with terrorism is not a battle against a religion. It is a battle against Islamic fanaticism. The world is filled with fanatics whether they are people like Dallas Cowboy fans who believe theirs is America's team, or fanatics that claim their denomination is correct and others will not be first in line for heaven, or even fanatics that stalk and want to be like their idols Justin Bieber or Miley Cyrus.

Bottom line, the world is filled with over-zealous believers of whatever it is they believe in. The difference is these Islamic radicals have taken their religion and turned it into a war. Islamic radicals will not accept anyone who believes differently, and if death is the answer to the infidel's problems, they will deal them death."

128

I popped open a can of iced tea and took a long drink.

"So, who do we target?" Ron asked.

Ron always wanted to cut to the chase and take the bull by the horn.

"I am afraid that answer is a bit more frightening than terrorism itself." Bernie chimed in. "We have reports that the Muslim brotherhood and other Islamic groups have infiltrated the United States and are poised to bring down our way of life from the inside."

"Give me names."

Ron walked over and picked up my can of iced tea and finished it off. Bernie continued.

"It is not individuals per se, but there are a great number of organizations operating in the United States that are openly Islamic and Muslim but covertly provide funding, manpower, and guidance to terrorist organizations." Bernie continued.

"Our efforts to infiltrate these organizations have proven worthwhile. We have had success in identifying, as I mentioned the other day, the financial and command and control center for all terrorist activity in the U.S."

"Where is that location?" Ron walked over to the refrigerator. He did his best thinking while seemingly distracted.

"The main concentration of communications is going in and out of Chicago and Detroit."

Bernie looked over to Ron

"Hey, toss me an apple will you?"

"If we know the companies and the city, why haven't we frozen their funds?"

Vance got up and walked to the refrigerator.

"I'll tell you what guys and gals, why don't we have some lunch first. It has been a long night and I, for one, could use some food. Maybe we can talk Biff into whipping up some vittles for us. After all, this is his new hometown." Bernie gave me a wink.

"Sure thing, Bernie, I would love to."

I stood up and Sara and Aga also sprang into action. I found an assortment of beef and pork chops in the fridge and plenty of vegetables. Aga went into the pantry and pulled out a bag of rice and some beans while Sara was pulling out a container of Green Chile (a New Mexican export and only worth getting if it is from New Mexico) and stared at it with great curiosity.

"Hey Ron, why don't you take the rest of the team out back and get some target practice in. I only need about thirty minutes. I will feed you guys better than ol' Rachel Ray could ever dream about doing in thirty minutes." I laughed alone realizing I must have been the only Food Network nerd in the group.

"Got it boss." Ron was up and out as Aga was hollering to him to get with the security guys for access to the gun shed.

"He has lot of energy." Aga said. "How did you two meet?"

"Oh he has been a friend for years. We were in the 7th Infantry Division together. We sort of had a mishap during an air assault demonstration and it kind of brought us closer together."

"What kind of mishap?" Sara jumped in.

"We sort of fell out of a helicopter." I grabbed a knife and started to trim the rib roast separating it into fairly decent sized ribeye steaks.

"You fell out of a helicopter?" Sara was laughing

"That must have hurt." Aga added.

"We survived."

I turned on the stovetop grill and brushed olive oil onto the grill surface.

"The Army sent him to Korea, and I got sent to a school in Virginia. After that, well, we lost touch until we were put on an assignment to retrieve some stuff in Alaska."

I seasoned the ribeye steaks with salt and pepper and did the same with the inch thick pork chops. The grill was just right so I brushed it with olive oil again and placed four chops and two of the ribeye steaks over the fire to cook.

"What do you think is going to happen?" Sara was cleaning some mushrooms and washing the green Chile's to throw on the grill as I had asked her to do.

"Well, Sara, I figure the steaks will stay on about five to seven minutes so we can have them at a medium rare…"

"No Biff," she started to laugh but her tone quickly snapped back to one of great concern and a bit of fear, "I meant with this terrorist movement here in our own backyard."

"Over the past couple of weeks I was sitting at home looking at the raw intelligence coming across the myriad of news reports and blogs it was easy to shake my head with frustration knowing that this was only twenty-five percent of the real story. Americans are unaware of the danger they are in because they depend on the media to give them the absolute, no-holds-barred truth. And the news agencies just can't do that."

"Why can't the news and media tell Americans the truth?"

Aga looked frustrated.

"This sounds too much like the days when Poland was really afraid of a Soviet invasion. No one told us the truth."

"You're right, Aga. It is the same. But the media cannot tell us everything because most of it is classified and even those in the Department of Defense or the Intelligence Community aren't fully aware of the one-hundred percent truth. And just like the Soviet Union back in the day, the media has an agenda to bring down our nation. And no, I don't say that with a disgruntled arrogance or as a 'war-mongering conservative' as I had been labeled. I say it as a realist who sees the media lying just to make one political party look better than the other. No specific party, mind you, just the one that they do not agree with for that season."

"So, what you are saying is that they will only report things that will help them look good?"

Sara walked over to smell the green Chile's that I had just placed on the grill with the steaks.

"I think it is more sinister than that. In Russia the number one news agency was Pravda. They became number one because they were basically the mouth piece for the government. If the government can control the media, freedom is lost."

"So what can we do?" asked Sara.

Sara stepped back as one of the ribeye steaks splattered indicating I needed to remove them from the grill and replace them with the other two steaks while flipping the pork chops over.

"Find the master minds and take them out. Sever the serpent at the head and it will not bite us."

"That is easy to say Biff," Aga brought the mushrooms to the stove and placed them in a pan with butter to start the sauté process. "We did this in Poland after the Berlin Wall came down. We have been nervously looking to the East ever since."

"Yes Aga," I acknowledged, "this is going to change America forever. We will never be a trusting nation. Never again."

We stood there in silence until we heard the beep of the rice cooker Aga had started. Amazing how twenty-five minutes could fly by. I took the pork chops off and placed the roasted green chilies on the cutting board where I diced them up before placing them into the pan with the mushrooms.

Aga scooped the rice into a serving bowl. I removed the last two ribeye steaks from the grill. Sara started to make gravy in the mushroom pan.

"Wow!"

I looked at the food. Looked at my watch. Looked at the two ladies.

"Thirty minutes exactly."

"I think we are in the wrong business, Biff," Aga smiled, "let's open up a restaurant."

We all laughed and the rest of the team started to come in for lunch.

"Smells good, Biff." Vance walked over and gave me a pat on the back. "I think if this thing with Prudencia doesn't work out, I may have to introduce you to my sister."

"Not in the cards my friend" I laughed and carried the tray of meats to the table.

"Wash up boys" Aga hollered. And they did.

We sat at the table looking at the food knowing that some tough times were coming. But for now, seize the day was the order of the moment.

"Biff," Aga looked at me and grabbed my hand, "can you say a prayer for our meal?"

We each reached and grabbed the hand of the person to either side of us and held our heads down.

"Lord, for what we are about to receive, we thank you. For what we are about to embark on, we ask you to protect us."

"Amen."

"Amen."

"Amen."

"Uhm, Biff?"

"Yes Ron?"

"Ain't we got any biscuits?"

SECRETS REVEALED:

WORSE THAN WE THOUGHT

Days passed and we went our separate ways to work individually on possible scenarios to address the problem of terrorism in the United States. Bernie sought approval by the Director of Intelligence Operations (DO) at the CIA to form this task force and promptly named our team Terrorism, USA. The DO nixed the name and gave us a classified name, but we agreed we would keep Terrorism USA as our internal name.

The teams would send each other situation updates or intelligence summaries as they completed their cursory look at the terrorism situation in their assigned region.

TERRORISM IN THE NORTHEAST:

Sara's research painted a damning picture of how terrorism was taking over the Northeast United States. The self-proclaimed epicenter of intellect, the northeast was becoming the center of terrorist plotting and planning. Most Americans believe the terrorist attacks on the World Trade Center towers were an isolated incident against America that involved foreign terrorists who came in, held a meeting, and then put their plan into action. The facts: The attacks of 9-11 were well planned and could have been much worse had it not been for one flaw in their plan: Time zones.

Intelligence after the fact revealed that plans for taking over planes in St. Louis, Denver, San Francisco, Los Angeles, and Seattle were in place but, all flights had been grounded and the attackers never even boarded their planes because they were not sure on whether the attack was to be a concerted effort based on the time in the Eastern Time Zone or a rippled effect event of terror with attacks staggering in one hour increments across the U.S.

Most people would say this was ludicrous, but one only has to point to the news reports of the day and intelligence released in 2011 detailing the LAX and DCA mock-ups found in certain Central American countries known to support terrorism and socialism (Venezuela).

The truth about terrorism in America is that there is a robust recruiting effort by al-Qaeda and other cells in full swing across our country reaching out to liberal minded students from the Ivy League and other major colleges and universities.

The Massachusetts Institute of Technology is a prime target with al-Qaeda experiencing success in recruiting some of America's brilliant minds to design weapons of terror and mass destruction. Recently, a grad student had developed a drone capable of delivering a large payload that was originally intended for use by the United States Postal Service (USPS). This student was initially contacted and recruited by al-Qaeda while attending Northeastern University. Over the years these recruiters courted him, coddled him, and, in essence, brain-washed him and brought him into the jihadist faith which built his hatred towards all things non-Muslim.

His drone then became a weapon in which the terrorists would pack full of explosives and target the Capital Building in Washington D.C. and the Pentagon. Fortunately, a special task force spearheaded by the FBI intercepted some of his communications and were able to insert themselves into the equation. According to Sara's research, an affidavit written by the FBI Special Agent in charge quotes the student as saying *"I just can't stop; there is no other choice for me. This is what we have to do. This is the righteous way … to terrorize enemies of Allah."* The student also said he would obey his calling to cause pain and even the deaths of any kafir — the Arabic term for nonbeliever.

During the investigation leading to his arrest, federal officials posing as al-Qaeda said that at no point did this man have sole control of explosive materials, such as C4, or guns, and that he was closely monitored by the FBI during his alleged plotting over the year. What he did have was the blue prints and the self-developed plan of attack. Just to make sure they had the right guy, they repeatedly questioned him about his plans which he improved upon and reiterated that he was committed to carrying out the attacks.

Prosecutors say that the student modified mobile phones to act as electrical switches for improvised explosive devices. He gave eight of them to the FBI undercover agents. According to the affidavit, when told that one of his devices had killed three U.S. soldiers and injured at least four others in Iraq, he exclaimed, *"That was exactly what I wanted."*

Prosecutors said that this young man had already hatched a plan to attack federal buildings before he met the undercover agents the year prior. He traveled to Washington, D.C. and took pictures of the Pentagon and the U.S. Capitol. The undercover team gave him at least $7,000 to purchase one of the remote-controlled planes he had designed and built. Each plane was the size of a human body. As agreed, the agents delivered twenty-five pounds of C4 military grade explosives, three grenades, and six AK-47 assault rifles to his apartment. His plan was to recruit other men to shoot at people fleeing the Pentagon, prosecutors said.

This was just one of at least twenty cases Sara uncovered. Boston is one of sixty-four urban metropolitan areas that have been designated by the federal government as "high-threat and high-density" with regard to acts of terrorism. Since the September 11, 2001 terrorist attack on New York, there has been several major alleged terrorist plots thwarted that were to take place in Massachusetts. Attacks were planned at sporting events, and an alleged shopping mall bombing plot was planned that involved U.S. citizens who wanted to join al-Qaeda.

Shocking as that may sound; Sara also uncovered a group of law students that were volunteering their time to advise al-Qaeda members on circumventing laws and taking full advantage of their "rights as Americans" or their "rights as foreign students here on student visas."

These students would hold weekend study sessions in buildings rented by the Islamic Society of North America (ISNA). At these meetings attendees were provided with meals, clothing, and any legal advice they needed. The focus of the seminars included an extensive look at an individual's rights under the Fourth Amendment which "prohibits the unreasonable search and seizure of personal property." The class was said to emphasize the right to freedom and privacy. It showed how to identify areas in your home as religious sanctuaries so that you can claim unlawful search infringing on your religious practice. It also covered, at length, exclusionary rules and the warrant requirement.

One seminar was taught on the importance of living the life of a Muslim in America and how to discredit all non-believers despite the First Amendment to the United States Constitution or any rule regarding freedom of religion. The students were taught that their Muslim faith overrules the amendment. It was imperative for all attendees to understand their mission: to make the world a Muslim world or a caliphate. The Islamic Caliphate guarantees religious freedom under the conditions that non-Muslim communities accept *dhimmi* (second class) status. In the U.S. this would mean forcing Christians, and those of the Jewish faith to either accept Islam or become servants of the same.

These classes were tremendously popular and identified as one of the greatest tools in converting non-Muslims. Two attorneys taught the classes and they were so popular that they were moved to Chicago where they began to help the Chicago area terrorist groups and inserted themselves into the Chicago political scene.

TERRORISM IN THE MIDWEST:

Vance blew us away with the Midwest report that tied in with Sara's information on the growing recruitment effort in Chicago but also extending from Milwaukee to Cleveland with a great concentration of recruits living in and around Detroit.

When we think of terrorism we think of Hamas, al-Qaeda, and the Taliban. We do not realize that many of the terror groups are hiding in plain sight – thanks to political correctness. The Palestine Liberation Organization or PLO is a terror group that current political administrations have accepted as legitimate entities and are even trying to grant the organization statehood. The same with the Muslim Brotherhood, which is nothing more than the headquarters for all Muslim things that are bad – they are the driving force behind the effort to insert sharia law into the United States Judicial system.

We rarely think of the terror movement hitting Mid-America and specifically iconic cities like Minneapolis. Vance informed us of an extraordinary recruitment effort of young men for terror organizations operating in and around Somalia. Recruiters have infiltrated a well respected mosque in the twin-cities area and many young men have disappeared after attending events at the mosque. The young men, actually boys ages 10 to 18, are being recruited to serve in the terrorist organization known as Al-Shabaab. The official name of this terrorist organization is Harakat al-Shabaab al-Mujahedeen (HSM) and is listed as an Islamic militant group under al-Qaeda that raises young men for the sake of holy war. So successful is their recruitment effort that for the first time ever a U.S. citizen was used as a suicide bomber in Somalia. This is not a record we need to be proud. Somali's fled their country to escape the growing violence against Christians and other non-conformists. Many came to the United States, but the reach of the terror organizations respect no borders.

Members of the U.S. Senate tried to figure out ways to stop this senseless violence with Joe Lieberman leading the way: "This is the most graphic and clear evidence that we've had thus far of a systematic campaign of recruitment of American youth, and in some ways the most promising of American youth, to leave the country to go fight a war that really will bring them to no good."

The Senator is correct, but the problem is greater than he could have ever imagined. The New York Times once declared that dozens of Americans were killed in Somalia while participating as al-Shabaab members. The al-Shabaab is the mujahedeen youth movement of jihadists or terrorists operating in Somalia. As of 2011, the group's foreign recruitment strategy was listed as extremely active in the United States, where members attempted to recruit from the local Muslim communities. According to an investigative report by the U.S. House Committee on Homeland Security, al-Shabaab have recruited over 40 Muslim Americans since 2007.

Foreign aid to these terrorist groups is not limited to the U.S. Of the foreign members, the former head of MI-5 (the United Kingdom's domestic counterintelligence and security agency), addressing a London security conference in 2010, advised that "a significant number of U.K. residents" were training with al-Shabaab. He also suggested that since Somalia, like Afghanistan, at the time had no effective central government, the presence of foreign fighters there could inspire terrorist incidents in the United Kingdom. "*It is only a matter of time before we see terrorism on our streets inspired by those who are today fighting alongside al-Shabaab.*"

The actual number of U.K. residents joining the fight has been estimated at between fifty and one-hundred persons; one source estimating around sixty active al-Shabaab recruiters, including forty Somalis and an additional twenty mainly British-based individuals who are believed to have ties with the group. There is also evidence of funding the group by Somalis residence in Britain with strong financial ties to banks and companies in the U.S., specifically Chicago.

Within his research, Vance identified Chicago as being the financial hub for terrorism activity with the U.S. and around the world. Most funding of terrorism efforts are open donations given to "dual-identity" organizations. In other words, you may think you are giving to an organization that will feed the homeless, but the same company supports the feeding of those training for terror purposes.

Other financial support comes in the form of money laundering and covert funding. Three educational charities in the United States are under investigation for their role in funding terrorist activities. Those charities: Muslim Youth of North America, Muslim Students Association of the U.S. and Canada, and Association of Muslim Scientists and Engineers. These groups are currently battling in the courts with the ACLU on their side. This is preposterous. The money coming through these organizations provided scholarship to known terrorists to earn their pilots license.

These organizations have been in the United States since the mid 1960's and have a presence on almost all major college campuses. There are no strict club bylaws that force the groups to follow the same rules, but instead, they are encouraged to branch out with different activities as needed to help in the recruiting of other students with 'special gifts and talents'. The only major goal is the establishment of the Islamic caliphate in the U.S.

The most troubling information provided by Vance leads to a financial path that is chilling. It begins with the

North American Islamic Trust (NAIT) which is a Saudi-backed organization based in Indiana. NAIT owns Islamic properties and promotes Islamic endowments in North America. It is the financial arm of the Muslim Students Association.

NAIT finances and holds titles to mosques, Islamic schools, and other real estate to safeguard and pool the assets of the American Muslim community, it develops financial vehicles and financial products that are compatible with both Shari'ah and American law, publishes and distributes Islamic literature, provides legal advice to Muslim organizations, and facilitates and coordinates Islamic community projects as well as funds the efforts of community organizers in major metropolitan areas.

In 2007, NAIT was named as an unindicted co-conspirator in the Holy Land Foundation (HLF) terrorist trial. A federal grand jury in Dallas, Texas, returned a 42-count indictment against the Holy Land Foundation. Charges included: conspiracy, providing material support to a foreign terrorist organization, tax evasion, and money laundering. The indictment alleged that the Holy Land Foundation provided more than $12.4 million to individuals and organizations linked to Hamas from 1995 to 2001.

NAIT was a huge financial supporter of the Council on American-Islamic Relations (CAIR) who received almost five-million dollars for relief and development just prior to the 2008 presidential election when CAIR not only made a sizeable contribution to the Democratic National Committee (DNC) but was represented with a delegate to the convention. Not only was Hussam Ayloush a delegate at the convention, but the FBI turned a deaf ear and a blind eye to the teachings of Ayloush who, as a delegate for the State of California proclaimed his hatred of Jews calling them a Nazi state and professed to be pro-Palestinian.

Sadly, many Americans even watched the Executive Director of CAIR interviewed on television from the convention expressing his excitement of working with Democrats on their new political platform with regards to the Middle East.

I think Vance summed it up when he told us how disconcerting it was to see known terrorist supporters working with political figures to push an Islamic agenda. But that was nothing.

TERRORISM IN THE SOUTHEAST:

Bernie had Sanders looking into reports of growing threat of terrorism in the Southeast. You would think that Florida would be the last place to expect terrorist activity. But Sanders revealed information that was troubling because you never heard of any of it in the media. Since 1970, there have been 92 terrorist incidents in the Miami area alone. 65 of these attacks were bombings or attempted bombings. Others were murders of Cuban exiles for political reasons.

When we started to look at terrorism in the United States we were ready for Hamas, the Taliban, and al-Qaeda. What we did not realize was the terror being brought in at the hands of Cuban exile terrorists.

These terrorists have blown up ships in the Miami Harbor; they have placed bombs on Russian ships in Puerto Rico and in New Jersey. They have blown up an aircraft in the air, killing all 73 persons on board. They have placed a bomb on an airliner in Miami setting it to explode while the plane was in the air, full of passengers. They planted a bomb in a car owned by a former Cuban Senator killing him instantly. They have blown off both legs of the News Director of the largest radio station in Florida. In March of 1979, they placed a bomb in a suitcase which detonated as it was being placed aboard a TWA 747 bound from New York to Los Angeles. The passengers were already aboard the jet when the explosion occurred, injuring 4 baggage handlers.

It was shocking to read about these terrorist attacks that took place in the Sunshine State. But even more disturbing was the fact that these were not isolated incidences and there were many other reports of Middle East based terror organizations training in Florida and establishing a working relationship with water-borne narco-traffickers. Yes, Sanders found evidence that Hamas and al-Qaeda were working with drug smugglers on the use of boats to evade law enforcement.

TERRORISM IN THE SOUTHWEST

Ron stayed with me in Raton as we looked into the ugliness of terrorism spilling into the United States through our southern border with Mexico and the port facilities in southern California. We took the normal route by using my CIA credentials to meet with the FBI and the New Mexico State Homeland Security officials to see what they could share with us regarding the terrorism problem. However, knowledge to these agencies is power, and they did not want to give up any information. Suddenly Ron had a great idea.

"Hey, Biff, why don't we just head to the border and see the problem for ourselves."

"You know? That might not be a bad idea." I said.

Terrorism, U.S.A.

THE TREK

Ron immediately took the lead on planning our trek to the border of New Mexico and Mexico. I called Bernie to brief him on what Ron and me were about to do. He was impressed that we were willing to get a firsthand look at the border area and find if there was a movement of terrorists into the United States. And, of course, I once again bade farewell to Prudencia.

As promised, the FBI delivered my corvette to Raton and, as luck would have it, the Chevrolet dealer volunteered to detail the car for me. Of course the service manager also wanted to take a look at the modifications and additions of the onboard computer system. I told him I had a brother who was a computer geek and "pimped-my-ride."

We packed lightly and planned to pick up hiking gear down in El Paso. Ron started to tap away at the keyboard for the onboard computer brought up a map of the border area between New Mexico and Mexico.

"Look at this, Biff. We head down to El Paso, Texas and work our way west on four wheelers across the New Mexico Border."

The area he was pointing to on the map looked extremely barren. He pulled up the satellite image, and it confirmed my suspicion: it was barren! There was nothing west of El Paso until you came to the small New Mexico town of Columbus.

"Well let's take the back roads so I can visit the UFO crash site in Roswell." I said.

"Heck yeah! Maybe we can get alien tattoo's, Biff?"

"I don't think so, Ron."

I shook my head and grinned.

We traveled South on the winding roads that paralleled I-25. The beautiful mountains fueled my imagination as I thought about cowboys and Indians riding the plains. I could almost see a wagon train of settlers crossing the mesas and valleys. What an incredible life it must have been.

Once we crossed Interstate 40 heading south we entered into the deserts of the land of enchantment. There is nothing to see for 90 miles except the over-grown truck stop known as Vaughn and our first goal - the UFO mecca of Roswell. I insisted we stop in Roswell where we had lunch at an amazing food joint called Big D's Downtown Dive. The food (you knew I was going there) was incredible. I ordered the Big D's Green Chile cheeseburger and a side of sweet potato fries. Ron ordered the kitchen. He has the metabolism of a hummingbird. Before we left Roswell Ron insisted on stopping at the UFO Museum on Main and 2nd street to buy an alien T-Shirt. Tourists!

Once out of Roswell we moved south and then west through Artesia to pick up highway 70 into El Paso. I knew we would need better transportation if we wanted to get a good look at the border, so we sought out any place where we might be able to rent or purchase a couple of four wheelers. We visited a few stores and it became apparent that we would need a specialty store. Ron checked the computer and recommended we visit TEK Motorsports.

We followed the GPS directions and arrived at the sports store which boasted a mid-year sale on a front window sign. We got out of the car and had to stretch before walking in. We were impressed with their selection of ATV's and after about five minutes a gentleman approached us to see if we needed any help.

However, first things first, and when Mother Nature calls… we sought her out and asked for a bathroom. We spent what seemed like an hour explaining to the sales person that we were not joking, we were going to buy two four wheelers and we needed a truck to tow them to a hunting area. Clearly he did not buy our story, and eventually referred us to the manager. The manager was not too happy about being pulled away from whatever "important work" he was doing in the back room.

"Gentlemen, I am Hector Martinez. I understand we have a problem here?

His tone was very condescending and almost dismissive. So I decided to hit him with a quick almost full disclosure story of our hunt for terrorists.

"Can we meet somewhere private?"

I looked at Hector and looked at an office area that was to our left.

"We can go in there," he said.

Hector lead us to a sales office and I closed the door once we were inside.

"Look, I am not going to beat around the bush. I am Biff Baxter with the CIA."

I flashed the credentials to make it official.

"This is Ron Sheposh. Ron and I are going to survey some of the border area west of here, and we need some supplies. We will need two four wheelers, extra fuel, and

151

anything else you think we may need to survive." I looked him right in the eyes.

"Can you help us?"

"It's getting bad, isn't it?" Hector asked crestfallen.

"I have seen not only the Mexicans coming across, but I have also found some strange things out on my property."

"What kind of strange things? I asked.

"I called the sheriff's department and all they did was confiscate it and I never heard anything else, but I did take a picture of it."

He was scrolling through picture files on his phone.

"This is what I found. There are three pictures."

He handed me the phone and I held it so that Ron can look with me.

"What the hell, Biff! It's a passport from Lebanon."

Ron hit the nail on the head. Not only was it from Lebanon but it was still active. I grabbed a piece of paper and wrote down the name and all pertinent information from the pictures.

"I also found their bible." Hector offered.

"The Quran?" Ron asked.

"Yes sir."

A chill ran up and down my spine as I realized America's nightmare was real. Terrorists were entering our borders. I know, not everyone from Lebanon is a terrorist, but what kind of person crosses a border and loses his passport on open property.

"We used to worry only about drugs and guns coming back and forth. I have been trying to sell my place because I am afraid that sooner or later my luck will run out."

Hector stared at the wall and his face was emotionless.

"Well can you help us help you? Better yet, can you help us save America?" I held my hand out and he grabbed it to seal the deal.

"I can help you, but I can't just give you the equipment. I need to pay bills." He said almost apologetically.

"My friend, this is a government black card. Price is no problem. We are paying you full price."

"In that case, I can offer you two four wheelers with cargo baskets and extra fuel, food, and water. And if needed, I do have a truck in the back with a trailer to haul the ATV's."

I don't think the manager had ever handled a deal of this magnitude because he was trembling, but what the heck, it was CIA money and I had information to gather.

"Guys, let me give you one suggestion."

Hector took a serious tone as he inched closer and lowered the volume of his speech.

"You really need to take a guide with you, and I have the perfect scout for you. He can also act as security in case you cross into Mexico or run into trouble."

"Besides coyotes and rattlesnakes, what kind of trouble can we run into?" Ron asked Hector.

"I will let Kie fill you in. Give me a few minutes while I get my team to bring the truck around and load up the four wheelers. I'm throwing one in for Kie because if what you are telling me is true, I want you to find out all you can about the border crossings. My ranch is west of here about twenty minutes and as you can see by the pictures, we have had many uninvited guests."

Hector grabbed his cell phone and as he walked away he spoke in a language I was not familiar with.

I looked at Ron as we walked towards the front of the shop and he browsed for t-shirts and hats.

"Tourists!" I mumbled.

We walked outside and looked up at the sign on the front of the store – 'TEK Motorsports'.

As we sat on the curb in front of the store Hector came out with a couple of cold drinks and a huge gentleman that looked like he could crush me with a squeeze of his pinky.

"Here's some drinks. The guys are loading up two Polaris Sportsman 700's onto the trailer and a Honda TRX for Kie."

He pointed to the big guy with him.

"Kie, I am Biff. This is Ron."

He shook my hand and my shoulder almost popped out of its socket.

"I understand you want to look at possible hunting spots." Kie asked clearly not knowing the whole story.

"Biff I didn't know if I was allowed to…"

I interrupted Hector. I knew he hadn't told Kie the reason we were there.

"I appreciate that Hector. I will brief him."

I pulled Kie aside and started to talk to him about our mission as Ron went inside to pick out some shirts.

Kie agreed to help us but insisted on taking extra provisions. This meant we wouldn't start out until the next morning. After everything was loaded onto the truck at TEK, we drove out to Kie's home where we finished packing and settled in for the night after a great dinner compliments of the Kie family. Kie insisted on camping gear, extra food, and a mini-arsenal of weapons. All of which he had at his home out off of Pete Domenici Highway near the border.

We headed west the next morning with Kie driving us along the border and showing us known "unofficial" crossing points for immigrants. It was amazing how wide open and unprotected our border was. There was a fence but it was in great disrepair and there were places where anyone could easily walk in and out of Mexico. After traveling 120 miles, we pulled over to get a close up ground survey of the border area. The terrain had drastically changed and had become a bit mountainous. We were west of Columbus, New Mexico. We looked south and saw nothing but Desert Mountains. We walked along the border area looking for nothing in particular, but hoping for something to help us determine who was using this treacherous border region to mask their movement into the United States.

"Hey, Biff, looks like we have company."

Ron had walked ahead but now came to a stop and was pointing to the north.

A Customs and Border Protection vehicle was coming towards us at a fairly high rate of speed. As the vehicle came closer Kie placed his AR-15 on the ground and raised his hands.

"Do as I do gentlemen, and nobody will get hurt," Kie said matter-of-factly.

Ron walked back towards us pointing his AR-15 to the ground, holding it by the stock with his left hand while raising his right hand.

I raised my arms and after interlacing my fingers, placed my hands on my head.

The CBP officer stopped the truck within 10 yards of our position, opened the driver side door and from a defensive position trained his weapon on us.

"Officer we are American citizens." Kie offered up the alibi.

"What are you doing in this area?"

Kie looked at me. "You're on Mr. Baxter."

I took a step forward which drew the ire of the agent.

"Sorry. Sorry! I am working with the CIA. My credentials are in my right back pants pocket."

I dared not reach for them.

"Take three steps forward. Slowly. And then turn around."

I did as instructed.

"Now get on your knees and leave your hands on your head."

I complied; I wasn't in the mood to have my head blown off just yet. Meanwhile, the CBP officer was calling for back up on his radio.

I was on my knees for about five minutes when I heard the sound of another vehicle coming from a trail on the west. Once I was able to see the dust from the moving truck, the officer on the scene moved forward and searched my back pockets.

He secured my wallet from my right hip pocket and my credentials from my left pocket. The other vehicle had joined the scene and the officer also joined in the "ready to shoot us" posture.

"Mr. Baxter. Get up."

The officer leaned forward and helped me to my feet.

"They're clear Kelly." He hollered to the other officer. "Come on over here gentlemen."

We followed him to his vehicle, a white Chevy Tahoe with the familiar green CBP emblem plastered on the side. The inside was tricked out with radios and weapons racks.

"I'm Agent Scott Carney. This is Agent Miguel Ortiz. Gentlemen, what the hell is the CIA doing on my border?"

"Agent Carney. Agent Ortiz. Nice to meet you." I shook their hands and introduced them to Ron and Kie.

"Gentlemen, we are here on a sensitive mission. My team is researching possible ingress sights for terrorists. Intelligence reports indicate the border between Mexico and the U.S. is a major avenue for their movement. Is there any truth to this or is this all surprising to you?"

"Mr. Baxter." Carney smiled and looked at Ortiz who was also grinning ear to ear. "We get off shift at 1800 which gives us a good eight hours to scare the crap out of you with the truth. We are overwhelmed with refugees, immigrants, lost Americans, animals, and yes, even terrorists. And every time we report it to our bosses, they report it to the government. But nothing is done to stop the crossings or to reinforce us."

"And if you will notice," Ortiz jumped in "we travel in single man teams in these isolated areas. We are so undermanned that I am afraid every time I leave home that I will not make it back."

"How many of you are on shift right now?" I asked, concerned that what I was hearing was amazingly ignorant.

"I can't tell you that, but I can say Ortiz and I have to cover about one hundred miles of the border. Each."

Ortiz froze and held his hand up to hush us. We all froze in place and focused on our sense of hearing.

"Helicopter" whispered Ron "Sounds like a Bell 206. But it's coming from the south."

"Yeah, we better get out of here. How did you guys get here?" Carney asked.

"We have a truck about two miles…" I was cut off by Ortiz.

"Get your asses in the truck! Let's go!"

He started to run towards his truck with Ron close on his heels. Kie was already in Carney's truck, and I was running around to the passenger side as Carney got in and placed it in drive.

"What is going on?" I screamed above the noise of the truck flying across the rocky terrain.

"The other truck stopped" Kie hollered.

Carney made a sharp left turn and looked west to Ortiz's truck. "He's okay. Looks like your boy is picking up your rifles."

It was then that I saw the helicopter flying extremely low. Out of the side door a uniformed man was shooting in our direction.

"Shots fired; shots fired; Mexican military copter; US Airspace" it was Ortiz's voice over the radio.

Surprisingly there was no reply.

Carney drove us to where Kie had parked our truck and ATV's. He pulled his vehicle around and set up in a defensive position. We jumped out of the truck and waited for the showdown. But the helicopter had already left the area.

Ortiz slid into our location. Ron jumped out of the truck before it came to a stop. Rifle out and ready he seemed a little put off when we told him the threat was gone.

"What the hell was that all about" Ron asked.

"That was the Mexican military. This happens every now and then but not too often." Ortiz answered.

"You mean the real Mexican military is shooting at you or at someone nearby that has crossed into the states?"

I was astonished.

"Unfortunately the shots were meant to scare us away from the area. Every time they do this, more drugs come into the sector." Carney replied.

Ron and I looked at each other in stunned silence. Kie walked up, stood between us and put his arms around us.

"Look guys. I think your efforts are noble but now you have the Mexican military shooting at border patrol agents. I don't think terrorism should be your focus. I think you have a problem with a neighbor you think is your friend but they aren't." Kie looked at us, put his arms down and walked toward the border patrol agents.

"I'll make a fire, if you think it is safe to stay here for a few moments. I would like to brew a special tea for us. It is a tribal brew of chamomile, black cohosh and horseweed, it will be just what we need right now to bring some calm in to the situation."

"I think that's a good idea Kie. I'll help you get it going," said Ortiz.

Ortiz and Kie walked over to where our provisions were packed.

The sun was almost directly overhead. I looked at my watch; it was just a few minutes after 1 PM. There was no wind, the clear skies held no clouds, and the mercury was slowly making its way to the top of the thermometer. It was already an M&M melting 96 degrees.

Ron went over and grabbed our rucksacks and a shade shelter and brought them to an area near the vehicles. Carney and I helped set up the shelter and cleared off an area to build a fire for the tea. Kie brewed the tea and we sat around to hear more about these border incursions.

"There are many incidents that just don't get any attention once our leaders report them to higher ups."

Carney took the first sip of the tea.

"Why not?" Ron jumped in. "This is serious stuff. We were just attacked by a foreign military that was clearly in U.S. airspace. How can they ignore that?"

"It is not the first time this has happened Ron. And I am sure it won't be the last. Our chain of command prepares a weekly report for the routine activities on the border. But when something like this happens they immediately send a serious incident report to the department of homeland security. The last time agents were fired upon, like we just experienced, DHS responded by saying it could not be confirmed if the helicopter was in U.S. airspace, nor could they confirm it was Mexican military." Ortiz sounded dejected.

"The Mexican military comes across on the ground, too. We've witnessed many engagements all along the border." Carney shrugged his shoulders. "But what can we do? Our rules of engagement are to not fire at Mexican military."

"That's crap!" Ron shouted "Rules of engagement should be, if they point their gun at me they're dead. Case closed."

Kie reached into a bag and passed around some dried Mescal leaves and some venison jerky.

I grabbed a few pieces of the Mescal and asked the million dollar question: "Clearly no one in homeland security has a clue. But what about terrorists; have you seen any evidence that terrorists are crossing the border?"

Ortiz and Carney looked at each other with a grin. Not a grin associated with pleasure or joy, but one found on the faces of those experiencing disbelief or disappointment.

"The numbers of known terrorist crossings are few. But the evidence of terrorists crossing is astronomical." Carney admitted with defeat in his voice.

"Can you break that down for me? Can you tell me what kind of evidence you have seen of terrorist crossings?" I took a drink of the tea hoping for an immediate calming effect. The desert heat was incredible and my anxiety was adding to my discomfort but this tea clearly hit the spot.

The two agents shifted uneasily. Clearly this was not a topic they were comfortable discussing. After a few quiet moments a teary-eyed Ortiz spoke up.

"Two years ago we had a group of men trying to enter our sector. Our spotters saw them and I went to intercept. There is never a "routine intercept" and we always ready to expect the unexpected. It was still light out and I knew that other agents were on the way since I could hear the radio traffic. Confident back up would be there, I high-tailed it over to the ridge right over there." He pointed to a mountainous area southwest of where we were talking. His mouth was dry and Kie handed him some tea. He took a good drink and stared at the ground as he continued.

"I got to the area where I thought they would cross and ran into five men. They opened fire but I was the better shot that day. One of them was getting away and as I aimed to shoot he turned around and smiled. 'You will pay Ortiz' he hollered and jumped down a ravine. I lost him."

"He knew your name?" Ron jumped in.

"Not only did he know his name," Carney answered, "he knew where he lived. Later that week his house was broken into and his wife and newborn son were killed."

"Holy crap!" Ron was dumbstruck as was I.

"I am so sorry my friend. I can't even begin to imagine..." I was interrupted by Kie.

"Why do you still work this, then." He gestured around pointing to the desert area.

"If not us, then who?" Ortiz answered matter-of-factly.

"I don't mean to take away from this tragedy at all and I am truly sorry. However I need to get to the bottom of this. What makes you think this was a terrorist attack?" I felt almost ghoulish asking such a question, but I had to find the terrorist connection.

Ortiz walked to his truck and opened the tailgate. After rummaging around he came around with box. "They left this…"

I took the box and opened it. Inside was the unmistakable banner used by al-Qaeda. A black flag normally flown by Islamic extremists as a sign of brotherhood and unity. Under the flag was a note attached to a picture of Ortiz and his family clearly taken without their knowledge in front of the Border Patrol station – the note read: *we are always watching – AQA.*

A chill ran up my spine.

SECRETS REVEALED:

Terrorism, USA

Bernie made a few phone calls and then arranged for us to meet at the Marriott Fairfield Inn in **AN UNDISCLOSED**. He cautioned us to not talk to one another or acknowledge knowing one another if we happened to cross paths in the hotel. Our instructions were to check-in, get a good night's sleep and meet at the pool at 7:00 AM.

Ron and I had traveled together many times but as we landed at **AN UNDISCLOSED MAJOR AIRPORT** we went our separate ways traveling to the hotel in different conveyances. Something was wrong, and as I took the taxi from the airport I couldn't help but wonder what had happened. Bernie's phone call was cryptic and the security precautions were out of character for this kind of a meeting.

The next morning at breakfast we were all gathered in the same room yet no one acknowledged one another. We all sat in close proximity of one another due to the size of the room, and yet, it was a cold and troubling environment and the tension was so thick you could cut it with a knife.

One by one we stood and walked towards the pool. One by one we were escorted past the pool by four 'well dressed men' and loaded into a van. Bernie, already sitting in the passenger seat of the van, motioned for us to remain quiet.

Ron, Sara, Sanders, Aga, and I all sat in the van with Bernie not saying a word. Two of the 'well dressed men'

164

walked up to the van; one opened the driver side door while the other opened the passenger double door. They both had the same menacing look about them. Tall, dark hair, sunglasses, cheap J.C. Penney suit with military type black shoes and black ties. But all of that did not impress me as much as the Sig Sauer P-229 holstered under their coats and now made visible as an intimidation move no doubt.

"Ladies and gentlemen. We are with the **UNDISCLOSED GOVERNMENT AGENCY**. As of today, under orders of the President of the United States your association with the CIA or any other Intelligence agency is hereby terminated. We will be going back inside the building. You will follow us to a room where each of you will receive a "cease and desist" order barring you from participating in any intelligence operation regarding national security. Are there any questions?"

The goon at the sliding passenger door looked at us as if daring us to speak.

We all sat silently.

"Good. Follow me."

We followed the agent to room 114 where we were directed to stand along the wall until our name was called. Ron went first and after about forty-five seconds he came out looked at me and continued down the hallway. The last time he looked at me like that was when we found out the CIA had duped us and had attempted to have us killed. Next Aga was called into the room. She went in swearing in Polish and laughing as she produced her passport and claimed diplomatic immunity. It looked like this was falling apart on the **GOVERNMENT AGENCY** pretty quickly. I just had to laugh – but not for too long. She was gone for maybe a minute and then, she left the room, looked at the two guards who escorted us and said "goodbye you two monkey's butts."

She laughed hysterically as they stood there powerless. Aga then demanded the front desk clerk to call the police to file a complaint.

I was next. I looked behind me as Bernie stood there with his head hung low like a condemned man awaiting the walk to the electric chair.

"Bernie, relax, you've been in worse situations." I whispered to him.

He cracked a smile and shook his head.

"No one told you to speak. Get inside."

The agent reached as if to push me in to the room. My instincts moved me to push his hand away grabbing it and breaking his middle finger.

"And you my simian friend need to never try to touch a human again." I looked at Bernie to see him laughing.

I walked into the room and noticed the two other gentlemen waiting also wearing shoulder harnesses carrying P-229's. A stack of papers were strewn across one of the beds and file folders were placed neatly on the desk.

"Well, well, well! If it isn't Biff Baxter."

I turned to see the unexpected face of David Shelton.

"What is this all about Dave? Are you still working with the rogue CIA agent Tina Ferguson?"

"Biff you just don't know when to shut up do you?. You should have retired and left the spy business to the young guys. But now you have pissed off some very important people," he shook his head.

Dave walked over to the desk and picked up the file folder with my name on it and pulled out a sheet of paper.

"Here you go super spy. No need to read it because all it says is that you agree to drop all research on this ghost you are chasing and forget everything you have read."

He was only acting tough because he knew the hired guns would not hesitate to take me down.

"I am not sure what research you are talking about but who exactly have I angered? You? Tina?"

"You are in over your head Biff. There are things you do not need to know about and there are things the people of the United States do not need to know. When the time is right the president will let the people know."

"Know what? That he's part of the terrorist effort to destroy America?"

"Sign this Biff or these two gentlemen will make my dream come true and shoot you on the spot."

I turned around and looked at the two agents. One had a drugged, non-emotional stare; the other looked as if he was ready to throw up. I knew there was no way I could take them both out so there was only one thing to do.

I grabbed the pen and signed the paper. I put the paper in the folder and handed it to Dave pressing it against his chest.

"Why don't you and me just pick a spot in this great country and have a duel. You, me, and please invite Tina." I pushed him and started toward the door.

"Biff" Dave hollered "watch your back."

I walked out the door and saw Bernie still waiting. I also heard a commotion in the lobby. I walked quickly to see if Aga was in any trouble. Sara was there with Aga and Ron. A plain clothes officer and two uniformed officers were talking with them. Aga had her passport out showing it to the officers. Ron was on the phone and Sara was standing by with a note pad writing feverishly.

Ron motioned for me to come over. As I reached him he seemed to have had a revelation or epiphany of sorts.

"Yes sir, please speak to this police officer." Ron handed the plain clothes officer the cell phone.

"Biff, that is Poland's Ambassador to the United States. He is filing a formal complaint and he is about to tell the cops that no one can leave the building until the FBI gets here."

POP POP POP POP POP

Everyone dropped to the ground as the sound of the gunfire came from down the hall. The police officers drew their pistols and carefully made their way to a better vantage point. They called units that were outside to watch for anyone exiting the building.

I walked over to the plain clothes officer to give him some info. "Officer there is a CIA agent in there, his name is Bernie Griffin. He was in room 114 talking with a rogue agent, two secret service officers and two officers in the hallway."

The plain clothes got on his handheld and passed the information to the other officers.

"Roger sir, we have two bodies in the hallway."

"Morris and Hart at the side exit. We see the bodies. There is also a body in the doorway of Room 114."

"Okay." The plain clothes officer was taking charge of the situation. "Morris can you see Jackson at the far end of the hallway?"

"Yes, I see him and Perry."

"Good. On your command Morris, both teams move down the hall and see what else we have. We have a witness that confirms six personnel in that area. Two in the hallway, two armed in the room, two unarmed in the room."

"Any VIPs?"

"Armed personnel are from a government agency."

"10-4. Moving now."

The officers moved cautiously down the hallway stopping just short of the room.

"This is the police. Come out with your hands on your head." Morris shouted into the room but there was no response.

"Tell them to call for Bernie Griffin," I urged the plain clothes officer.

"Morris, possible victims name is Griffin. Bernie Griffin."

"10-4"

"Griffin, Bernie Griffin can you hear me?"

Still silence.

"Moving in. Follow me."

The officers moved in and cleared the room finding a fourth government agent down. There was an unidentified fifth victim laying under the table in the room. No other bodies found.

All areas of the room were searched. "No sign of a sixth person" was the message relayed to the plain clothes officer who turned to me and asked if I could come down and ID the bodies.

I told him I could and we walked down to room 114.

"These two are government agents," I pointed to the two bodies in the hallway. "This one is a government agent" the body was laying in the door way as if he tried to get out. It was the officer I saw that looked like he was going to throw up.

"Morris, these guys are still alive." Perry hollered the revelation and then got on the radio requesting medical support.

"That guy on the bed is from that same government agency and that one over there under the table is David Shelton. Rogue CIA."

I looked around puzzled as I walked toward Shelton. I nudged him with my foot (okay I actually kicked him).

"Hey loser. Who sent you? Who do you work for?"

Shelton looked at me with disgust. "You are a very lucky man. Tina told me not to kill you. She wanted you to be humiliated as a traitor once they arrested you for disobeying an executive order."

"What order is that?"

"The president is about to make it a federal crime to investigate terrorism on U.S. soil without oversight by DHS. Our day is coming and I cannot wait to see you put away in one of our detention centers."

"I can't wait to see you in prison ol' Davey boy."

I reached down to help him up but instead he pulled out a knife, swung at me and missed. He grimaced in pain and plunged the knife in his neck.

"Never Biff" he gasped "You... will... never...win. Allahu akbar."

"Morris! Perry! Anyone..." I hollered looking around.

Two paramedics had entered the room, pushed me aside and started working on Shelton to no avail. He had killed himself.

The police officers secured the weapons of the agents belonging to the government agency I was not allowed to name and started to interview them. I turned to the plain clothes officer who finally joined us.

"Officer I do not see Bernie Griffin."

"Well they told me they have searched the entire room. No one else seems to be here. We will start a room by room search once we get more units on scene."

I took another look around the room and noticed the files that had been on the table were missing. I looked over to the bed; those papers I had seen earlier were also missing. And Bernie was missing.

I taught him well.

SECRETS REVEALED:

Terrorism, U.S.A.

Final Analysis

Although officially we were not allowed to pursue our research on terrorism activity in the United States, no one said I couldn't continue my hobby of analyzing the news and putting together the puzzle of truth with the pieces of half-truths told to us by the media.

I am still not sure why our current administration has a problem with uttering the words "we are under attack by terrorists" because the truth is… we are. And we have been for at least fifteen years if not longer. History shows the planning or "reconnaissance" phase of this war waged by terrorists against the U.S. began back in the 1950's, and thanks to organizations like the ACLU and the Muslim Brotherhood and their countless law suits, these terrorists still have a foothold in our government and in our White House. The question now is 'how embedded is this terrorist presence?'

Records show us that at the end of President Harry Truman's second term in office, U.S. intelligence agencies considered using Islam to help in fight against Soviet Cold War influence. President Eisenhower took the step to invite members of the Muslim Brotherhood to the Oval Office prior to their conference on "Islamic Colloquium" held at Princeton University. The Muslim Brotherhood not only received support from the U.S. Department of State, but the meeting at the White House also served to cement U.S. relations with the group.[xii] The Muslim Brotherhood has since been a mainstay in the Washington D.C. inner-circles.[xiii]

There have been Muslim advisors for every president since the initial introduction of the Muslim Brotherhood to the nation by President Truman. Most presidents did not know the dangerous nature of this organization; and, as with most people in the 1950's and 60's their innocence or naivety could not allow them to believe that anyone would try to infiltrate our government.

More recently Karl Rove, a former adviser to George W. Bush, a political figure and an analyst I have a great respect for, also confirmed that the Bush administration was told to reach out to the Muslim Brotherhood in order to keep the U.S. population of Muslims from feeling isolated or left out. These meetings seemed to send a mixed message to the world. This move to bring together the two worlds, made it made it seem that the United States, the world's super power was endorsing an organization that was beginning to show their evil desires (this happened in 2005). Once the Egyptian Dictator Hosni Mubarak was kicked out, he demanded the U.S. stop speaking to this opposition group. The U.S. did just that and started to distance them from the Muslim Brotherhood.

Recent developments through the FBI confirm the existence of Muslim/Islamic entities operating in the United States. The FBI has determined these groups directly aid other terrorist organizations. These organizations include:

ISNA Fiqh Committee (now known as the Fiqh Council of North America)

ISNA Political Awareness Committee

Muslim Youth of North America

Muslim Students Association of the U.S. and Canada

Association of Muslim Scientists and Engineers

Islamic Medical Association (of North America)

Islamic Teaching Center

Malaysian Islamic Study Group
Foundation for International Development
North American Islamic Trust
Islamic Centers Division
American Trust Publications
Islamic Book Service
Islamic Circle of North America
Muslim Arab Youth Association
Islamic Association for Palestine
United Association for Studies and Research
International Institute of Islamic Thought
Muslim Communities Association
Association of Muslim Social Scientists (of North America)
Islamic Housing Cooperative
Muslim Businessmen Association
Islamic Education Department
Occupied Land Fund (later known as the Holy Land Foundation for Relief and Development)
Mercy International Association
Baitul Mal Inc.
Islamic Information Center (of America)

Throughout the years, the State Department has noticed a troubling trend in America: Islamic sympathizers and Muslim support was growing and young college students were being lured to the call of the Imam's to convert to Islam and join them in converting the world. Students were taking summer trips to Islamic camps both in the United States and abroad.

It is the same dilemma Great Britain is facing and as we grow closer to the all-out war against terror, we will see more and more people joining the ranks of terrorist supporters.

Records show that Barack Obama traveled to Pakistan in 1981. Although there were only a few travel advisories during that time issued for travel in that region, and travel there was not illegal, the strange fact is he never mentioned this trip in either one of his two books <u>Dreams From My Father</u> or <u>Audacity of Hope</u>.

Obama's mother, Ann Dunham is quoted as saying "Barry spent July in Jakarta, then went to Pakistan to visit a friend from Occidental College on his way back to the United States." As a point of interest, Ramadan, the official Muslim celebration begins around the third of July and lasts one full lunar month.

Not much has been made about Obama's trip to Pakistan, and on the peripheral, not much should be made about this trip. However, Obama raised the issue about this trip when he was challenging Hillary Clinton on her lack of foreign affairs knowledge. He claimed his trip to Pakistan illustrated his vast knowledge of the difference in the Sunni and Shia cultures.

Although no one really made a fuss about his trip, in March 2008, contract employees for the State Department were caught illegally breaching the passport files of the three main presidential candidates – Barack Obama, John McCain, and Hillary Clinton. The media made little fuss about this records breach, and in doing so, they ignored two very interesting points of this story:

1. This was the third time Obama's records were "uniquely" visited by special contractors whose access also included the ability to alter the records.
2. The CEO of one of the companies whose employees were accused of improperly looking at the passport records was a consultant for the Obama campaign.

Conspiracy Theorists cling to this search of records as an important fact to see if Obama's trip to Pakistan was recorded on a U.S. Passport. Their claim is that records show that in the 1980's and up until today many Americans travel to Pakistan, Afghanistan, Iraq, or Syria for the purpose of supporting terrorist organizations or enrolling in training to join the terrorism effort. Most of them use bogus passports and even travel to foreign countries, renouncing their U.S. citizenship and securing a passport from another country.

Bottom line: The tie in to terrorism (albeit a loose tie): The CEO of the company that conducted the illegal breach of the records was John O. Brennan, a key Obama adviser, and later Assistant to the President and Deputy National Security Adviser for Homeland Security and Counterterrorism.

I believe a terrorist invasion of the U.S. will come in a form we have never expected. I believe the offensive started with the preparation by the Muslim Brotherhood many years ago to insert one of their own into the White House. It took them years, but now they have one of their own (if not one that they own) sitting in the oval office.

I am not accusing the president of being a terrorist; I am accusing him of dereliction of duty as president and commander in chief. I am saying that whoever is advising him, or like we say in the HUMINT world, his handler is keeping the president on the sidelines while the terrorists invade the U.S.

There is a force that has been staging for these days when terrorist groups can operate freely in the land of their foes. Terrorists have set up shop here in America and are setting up for the greatest attack mankind will ever know. Terrorists are continuing to enter the United States with little to no repercussions for their illegal entry. Instead, many of the terrorists we have captured, whether on the battlefield, at our border, or on the tarmac, are not being treated as enemy combatants because our president and his administration refuses to call these people terrorists.

Terrorists have found fiscal shelters in one of America's largest cities, and ironically the city our President once called home – Chicago. Terrorists have recruited in colleges and universities along the east coast and throughout the Ivy League. Colleges that were learning institutions of Barack Obama and Eric Holder.

And what is next? Here is my best guess: While the whole world is pre-occupied with other events of the day, terrorists will make their move. While the U.S. is studying the ISIS advance in Iraq the terrorists will move against the United States. The world is worried about what to do about the destruction of Iraq and because all eyes are on the Levant and Maghreb regions of the world and no one is looking into the rapid move of terrorists into the U.S. with the exception of those who are in on the plan or those astute analysts that understand the mind of the terrorist.

Question: Why won't the president or the head of the DOJ check the situation on the U.S. / Mexico border?

Answer: They refuse to go because they know how dangerous it is and how deadly the border will become in a few weeks or months. This flooding of immigrants to the border is a staged movement by al-Qaeda to distract our border security while moving in two dangerous weapons to be used against Americans – Terrorists and drugs. The U.S. Government knew about the influx of refugees almost six months prior to their flooding the border as evidenced by a solicitation for Escort Services for Unaccompanied Alien Children dated January 29, 2014.[xiv]

Question: But what about the children; weren't they just fleeing persecution in a poor country?

Answer: Yes and no. These are very poor countries and some of the refugees are coming from some of the most dangerous cities in the world. However, it takes time to move these people from Guatemala to the U.S. border. Plenty of time for our intelligence community had to hear about the wave of humanity that was coming our way. Plenty of time for our President and his administration to react and stop the wave before it even came to our border.

As horrible as this will sounds, the truth is these terrorists do not care about the lives of these "expendable" children. The only use these children are to them is as a distraction to the front line of defense of the United States.

The United States MUST help these children. It is our moral obligation as a Christian nation. What has made this such a sensitive and heart-wrenching topic is the American citizen is now forced to do what they should have been doing all along: help the down-trodden. We are seeing Americans argue that we need to feed our own children and house our own homeless – Yes! But we should have been doing this long time ago. Guilt is a strange thing in that it acts as a reminder of the "right things" we should have been doing.

Question: How will the terrorists attack? And if they attack, where?

Answer: This is complicated. We know the terrorists will attack America because they have done it before and they have promised to do it again. They will attack. This is constantly debated among my friends in the intelligence community; they will attack by air, sea, and ground. We know that the operatives that live here in the U.S. can attack with car bombs, truck bombs, bus bombs or derail trains and hijack other modes of ground transportation because the materiel needed to conduct such attacks are readily available.

I contend they can also attack sea ports in order to allow ships to come to port that are possibly carrying more weapons or just attack the sea ports to isolate us and cripple our economy.

They can attack by air. They showed their ability to do it on September 11, 2001. Despite all the conspiracy theories, I know firsthand that the only reason the attack on America on September 11, 2001 was not bigger is one error in the plans of the terrorists. There was a plan in place to have a multi-city attack of terror. Targets included the cities of New York, Washington D.C., Los Angeles, San Francisco, and Las Vegas. The error? The U.S. has multiple time zones and their plans did not take this into consideration. But rest assured, the miscommunications from this first major attack will not be repeated.

One critical piece of intelligence that has been quietly shelved is the missing Malaysian plane. I know the media and their so called experts have said we will never retrieve that plane and that it is gone forever. And I would have to agree with that assessment. But if you think outside the box for just a minute you may conclude that the reason we will never see that plane again is because it is in the hands of terrorists and has been retrofitted to be a huge weapon of mass destruction. By now the terrorists have had ample time to strip the plane of all chairs and unnecessary equipment and retrofit the fuselage with explosives. The plane most likely has received a new paint job and all tracking systems have been removed. It is now a weapon of mass destruction that can fly from Pakistan to Washington D.C. with no problems. And by flying a giant bomb the terrorists have a win-win situation especially if the bomb is of a radioactive or nuclear nature. If the plane makes it to the target, they win, many will be killed and terror will reign victoriously. If the plane is intercepted by fighter aircraft and an order is given by another country to shoot it down, the terrorists still win as many people will be killed by the fall out and terror will reign victoriously. Bottom line: If that plane ever gets off the ground, many will die despite how the bomb is detonated.

As for where they will attack, that too is debated by the experts in the intelligence community. Some say targets will be strategic and include power stations, dams, refineries, etc. Others will tell you they want a body count and will select areas like Washington D.C. and most of the East Coast. I say an attack of this magnitude is a disaster wherever it takes place.

Question: What will it take to stop this from happening?

Answer: We can't stop it and the next two years will be the scariest years. I have heard some analysts say that there will be a "minor" terrorist attack in America that will allow the president to declare martial law and put the 2016 election on hold until the threat is gone. This, in effect, will destroy America and we will be a Muslim nation and there will be no returning to our original state without a revolution. Other analysts claim that should we experience no terrorist attack in the next two years, we have already left ourselves vulnerable because our military is currently being stretched thin because our government continues to reduce the numbers of military members in order to help our fiscal state. It is opined that rebuilding our military to a readiness level that will keep us safe will take ten to fifteen years and possibly include a mandatory conscription period early on to keep Russia or China from invading.

My final warning: over the past decades our liberties have been chipped away because many of our politicians are not looking out for the good of the citizenry, but for the good of their pockets. It is sad to know that special interest groups are running this country by buying these politicians. We have seen a push to take away our right to bear arms because special interest groups, and the media keeps telling us that guns are dangerous and kill too many innocent people. But July 4, 2014 proved all too well what tight gun restrictions will do for a civilized society. Chicago is a gun-free zone where honest citizens are forbidden to own guns. However, criminals are not honest citizens and they do own guns. They have killed 14, and over 80 other were shot… in a gun free zone on July 4, 2014.

Our freedom of speech is under attack too. Try to speak ill about Muslims and find yourself arrested. Our religious freedom is gone, unless you are Muslim. Our phone calls are monitored; every keystroke recorded as our 4th amendment rights are being erased. The only people we are allowed to speak ill about are Christians and southerners and if you don't believe me, just watch the evening news.

But our government officials do not care about the citizens of the United States. Most politicians will tell you they are looking out for the good of their constituents and when they speak these "inspiring words" I apply my litmus test and ask them to answer this simple question: how can we jump through hoops to help this wave of humanity crossing our border yet we cannot help the poor and homeless in our own communities? How is it that illegal's from Central America are now being housed in once empty buildings on military bases, yet veterans live in boxes on the side of the roads just outside of these same bases? Why is it that Republican Representatives tried to visit refugee holding areas in Oklahoma and Texas but were turned away by private security guards? And why is it that certain Democrat politicians are granted access to these same areas?

There is something amiss in Washington D.C. and I will be bold enough to say that it started decades ago with the push to remove God from every aspect of our existence. This is now compounded by Obama's "rebuilding of America" that terrorism in the USA is about to take place. Remember this, something that needs rebuilding needs to be torn down first. I truly believe events of our past will culminate in the Obama administration changing America to a point where we will no longer have freedom of choice but be forced to accept living in a country where we have NO freedom of choice. Since the Presidential administrations of the 1960's the biblical Christians or evangelicals have been muzzled and every attempt is being made to erase Christianity.

Our current President is a man with extreme prejudices that he has admitted: from his book <u>Dreams of My Father</u> – "*I ceased to advertise my mother's race at the age of 12 or 13, when I began to suspect that by doing so I was ingratiating myself to whites.*" And further on in the same book – "*I found solace in nursing a pervasive sense of grievance and animosity against my mother's race.*" And there is more: In <u>Audacity of Hope</u> he writes – "*I will stand with the Muslims should the political winds shift in an ugly direction.*"

So with that I leave you with these top six timeless quotes by President Barack Hussein Obama (nee Barry Soetero):

6. "Islam has always been part of America."

5. "Islam has a proud tradition of tolerance."

4. "As a student of history, I also know civilization's debt to Islam."

3. "We will convey our deep appreciation for the Islamic faith, which has done so much over the centuries to shape the world, including in my own country."

2. "The sweetest sound I know is the Muslim call to prayer."

1. "The future must not belong to those who slander the Prophet of Islam."

Good luck my fellow Americans. Enduring this assault by terrorists will be a tough journey. I wish you well.

Biff Baxter – OUT.

Terrorism, U.S.A.

RECOMMENDED READING:

The Vigilance Project: An Analysis of 32 Terrorism Cases Against the Homeland; New York State Intelligence Center – December 2010

Hezbollah: Portrait of a Terrorist Organization; The Meir Amit Intelligence and Terrorism Information Center, December 2012

Islam and the Need for Western Vigilance; The Brussels Journal, July 2012

The Influence and Implications of Terrorist Ideology in Commercial Aviation Targeting; ACC Threat Information Fusion Cell, September 2012

Targeting Tomorrow's Terrorist Today (T4) Through Open Source Intelligence (OSINT); E.B. Benavides, February 2009

Beware of Imitators – al-Qaida through the lens of its Confidential Secretary; Combating Terrorism Center at West Point, June 2012

ABOUT THE AUTHOR:

Willis "Biff" Bullard has over 20 years military intelligence experience and 5 years of civilian research analysis experience and a few years doing things he can't tell you about. His military experience ranges from office and security management, operations and training for US Opposition Forces (OPFOR), to field operations in Europe, South America and the Middle East. Many of his intelligence assessments have been instrumental in affecting foreign policy and tactical missions planning decisions. Mr. Bullard's analysis was also sought out by the civilian sector with some of his works being published in Jane's Defense Magazines and other periodicals. He also served as a Senior Operations Analyst for a major government contractor working on special programs for TSWG and OSD.

Mr. Bullard is fluent in Spanish with a working knowledge in German and had begun Arabic training prior to his retirement.

Mr. Bullard now lives a quiet and low stress life with his wife of about 100 years in the Land of Enchantment – New Mexico. Together they are watching their two children excel in the paths of life God has directed them.

i Several Studies point to this topic. See A Line in the Sand: Countering Crime, Violence and Terror at the Southwest Border. A Majority Report by the US House Committee on Homeland Security, November 2012

ii Multiple studies on future terrorist attacks on U.S. soil. See A Pakistan-based Terrorist Attack on the U.S. Homeland, Council on Foreign Relations Press, August 2011

iii Extensive news coverage. See ISIS Parades Scud Missile 'Heading Towards Israel', Israel National News, July 2014

iv Border Crossings and Terrorist Attacks in the United States: Lessons for Protecting against Dangerous Entrants, National Consortium for the Study of Terrorism and Responses to Terrorism, University of Maryland, November 2012

v Multiple reports and formerly classified documents exist. See Flight 800 Investigation, Associated Retired Aviation Professionals, 1997

vi The Audacity of Hope, Barack Obama, Text Publishing Company, October 2006

vii The Influence of Islamic Law on Intelligence and Law Enforcement, The Vanguard: Journal of the Military Intelligence Corps Association, Vol 16, January 2011.

viii The Guide to Understanding Islam – The Politically incorrect truth about Islam. By Religion of Peace Inc., 2006

ix Government Exhibit 003-0085, 3:04-CR-240-G, U.S. v HLF, et al. Bate# ISE-SW/1B10

END NOTES:

[x] Ibid

[xi] Multiple sources used – see 39 Principles of Jihad, J.D. Halevi, Intelligence and Terrorism Information Center at the Center for Special Studies (C.S.S.)

[xii] A Mosque in Munich, by Ian Johnson, Houghton Mifflin Harcourt

[xiii] In Search of Friends Among the Foes. The Washington Post

[xiv] Federal Business Opportunities: Solicitation Number BERKS-RFI, January 29, 2014.

www.ingramcontent.com/pod-product-compliance
Lightning Source LLC
Chambersburg PA
CBHW070110290526
45789CB00005B/1988